Thunders and Comforts

A Bible Study on Jeremiah: Leaders' Notes

Eunice Kwok

Thunders and Comforts:
A Bible Study on Jeremiah (Leaders' Notes)

ISBN: 9798829103781

Cover design by Eunice Kwok

DEDICATED TO

The Garden Hut Girls,

Barbara, Claire, Florence, Heather,
Joanna, Lin, Ruth, Sarah, and Sheena,

my dear sisters in Christ
whom I have been honoured to serve
in the bible study group context.

This work is a fruit of our fellowship.

.

Contents

PREFACE

This study was first written in the spring term of 2022 for the ladies' fellowship group that I co-lead. Preparing bible studies for small groups is a challenging and time-consuming task that not many can comfortably afford to take on. It is therefore popular to rely on readily prepared resources for small group studies, which may or may not come with leaders' notes. Even if leaders' notes are included, the answers are often directional rather than comprehensive. Most bible study groups follow the school term structure which imposes a further constraint on the optimal length of a study to range from 8 to 12 sessions. Needless to say, some books of the Bible fit into this format better than others, resulting in a commonly observed knowledge gap of the Bible on the hefty books in the Old Testament, which in turn hinders our understanding of the New Testament. To fit into the specified format, we often know them by their most cross-referenced verses /chapters in the New Testament, or approach them by some selected themes. This is at odds with interpreting the bible texts in context, and poses difficulty for those leading or attempting the studies. In addition, there is much insight to be gleaned from tracing the progression through a book. This emphasis on the continuity of a book is inevitably missed by a selective study approach.

As leaders gathered at the end of each term and discussed, among other things, the next study for each group, Isaiah was suggested. But it had previously been studied multiple times in the living memory of the existing members. I thought why not Jeremiah? No one seemed to have studied it before. As we looked into it, we could not find a ready-made study we could use. This might have explained why it had not been studied before. Rather than being a reason for not studying Jeremiah, it was a reason to study it all the more! To make this happen, I undertook this ambitious project of writing the bible study myself for the group, one that covers the whole book of Jeremiah and traces its progression, with its pulse and subject matters dictated by the texts rather than by some preset themes. At the end of the study, we shall at least know the whole contents of Jeremiah rather than its disjointed bits and pieces.

With its stress on the continuity of the book, this promises to be an exciting journey, whereby sound of thunders is mixed with sound of consolation. There will be ruin and destruction before planting and building, striking before healing. Among all the upheavals, God's faithfulness to His covenant and people is as sure as the law of the universe which faithfully stands today as God has always appointed. We meet God as the Judge but also the loving Father with His tender mercy. His patience in His instruction to His stubborn and rebellious children is tireless while His guidance and counsel to Jeremiah is wise and tender. Jeremiah is so honest with his struggles that we see Jeremiah in the making as well; this growth pain of a Christian is highly relatable to our own experience. While we get acquainted with the prophecy of Jeremiah and Jeremiah the Prophet himself, there are surprisingly many treasures to glean for our daily walk in Christ. If you allow God's Word to minister to you, this will be a soul-searching and convicting journey for you.

As it was an ambitious project to write, it is an ambitious endeavour to study it. Like hiking, it will take some effort to gain the view and there is no shortcut. I envisage that preparation will take longer than what we are used to. Reading through the bible text alone may take one sitting while attempting the questions may take one or two sittings, depending on how much you would like to ponder over them. Each question specifies the verse references to help you narrow down the focus and efficiently navigate through the extensive text to get an overview. There are short questions as well as long questions, which are indicated to members by the spacing that I leave them in the accompanying study guide, available separately.

In this study, you will encounter "more questions" than your usual expectation, which may seem overwhelming. If I can somehow show you the highlighted texts, I suppose there would not be as many questions. A lot of the questions are fact-finding with the purpose to highlight the texts and prepare us for the discussion questions. Discussion without grasping some details is very hard (like thinking in a vacuum). In contrast, once we have grasped some details, the conclusions drawn are brought forth almost effortlessly because they flow naturally from the text. This is *seeing*. With a big chunk of text, I believe pointers are helpful to guide the thoughts. If the study only has discussion questions without the guiding questions that work through the text, questions are fewer but I imagine few will be able to attempt them – this will be a hugely frustrating study experience. I am not saying this is the right way or best way or the recommended way; rather, I am only explaining myself why the study takes the form it is. Given that exposition means to *bring out of the text what is there and expose it to view*,[1] it is important that our discussion points are seen connected to the text. In addition, personally I believe that familiarizing ourselves with the Bible texts is a merit in its own right because they are the root of all insights and memory of the raw texts allows the Spirit to recall them later on to give us further insights. I don't

---

[1] John Piper, *Expository Exultation: Christian Preaching as Worship*, Crossway 2018, p. 52, citing John Stott.

think our discussion has similar richness and depth. This is why God's Word is living!

Covering 52 chapters in 12 sessions is sweeping, so we can only manage a birdseye view, which will be a valuable foundation should you wish to dwell into any area more deeply in your own time. Preparation before the group meeting will certainly enhance the group learning experience. But the study has been written in such a way that group members who have failed to complete the preparation beforehand will still be able to get something out of the session. So encourage them to come along. That said, please bear in mind that you most likely won't have time to read through the full text during the session because of its length. It will be helpful if members have at least read through the assigned texts before each group session.

Applications are drawn out either at the end or along the way as the Spirit leads! You may find not having time to discuss most of them but they are valuable for individuals' private meditation of God's word continuously. I have prepared a bonus session at the end to help the group digest what have been learnt and discuss personal applications, should you find that helpful.

I make my leader's notes publicly available because I know how much work it costs to prepare it and the frustration that the less resourceful leaders must have. I pray God will use it as an instrument to lessen your load, and give you more confidence in your role of edifying your group members with God's Word and fostering their spiritual growth. Rather than trying to hit *my* answers provided here, let it be a collective experience of seeking the <u>mind</u> of God spoken through His Word - this is our real objective.

References that I have consulted in preparing this study are as follows:

- *Knowing the Bible: Jeremiah,* by Matthew S. Harmon, Crossway;
- Matthew Henry's commentary;
- Calvin's commentary,

- Reformation Study Bible notes,
- Calvin's *Institutes of the Christian Religion*,
- Martyn Lloyd-Jones' *Great Doctrines of the Bible*, Crossway.

Writer's jitters are common and real. What is my qualification to commend this work to you? I have none. But the Bible says: *Such is the confidence that we have through Christ towards God. Not that we are sufficient in ourselves to claim anything as coming from us, but our sufficiency is from God, who has made us competent to be ministers of a new covenant* (2 Cor 3:4-6). When comes to a word ministry, who can claim confidence in oneself indeed? If we only focus on our inadequacies, we will be frozen in a spirit of timidity which produces perennial inaction. Apostle Paul encourages Timothy: *For this reason I remind you to fan into flame the gift of God, which is in you through the laying on of my hands, for God gave us a spirit not of fear but of power and love and self-control* (2 Tim 1:6-7). As I am a work-in-progress, this work inevitably is too. What I can commend to you is the sincere effort and diligence in preparing this work given the time frame. As I laboured at my desk, it was an attempt to love my God with all my heart and with all my soul and with all my mind and with all my strength (Mark 12:30), and this output, I pray, could serve as a window for you to glimpse God's Truth. Wherever it falls short, may God make your learning experience complete with His grace. Amen.

May this work bring all who study it a deeper knowledge of God, an enhanced love for His word and strengthened resolve in your perseverance!

Eunice Kwok
May 2022

Thunders and Comforts

SESSION ONE

Jeremiah 1 and 2 Kings 21-25

Why study OT prophecy?

And we have something more [than being eyewitnesses of the transfiguration of Jesus], *the prophetic word, to which you will do well to pay attention as a lamp shining in a dark place, until the day dawns and the morning star rises in your hearts, knowing this first of all, that no prophecy of Scripture comes from someone's own interpretation. For no prophecy was ever produced by the will of man, but men spoke from God as they were carried alone by the Holy Spirit* (2 Pet 1:19-21). It is mind-boggling that in our hands is something better than being eyewitness of Jesus' transfiguration, an event of a lifetime that I am sure we would have dropped everything to witness if we could. And yet the prophetic word we are going to study is more. Do we see it that way with the Word of God? Pray that God leads us on this journey to find out how this is so.

I. The historical background

When did Jeremiah commence his office as a prophet (v2)? He started his public ministry in the 13th year of Josiah's reign in Judah, i.e. 626 BC. [NB: son here denotes successors rather than a biological relationship.] **When did it end?** It ended when Jerusalem was captured and Judah went into exile in 586 BC. Relative to Isaiah, Jeremiah began his public ministry many years after Isaiah whose ministry was in the 700s BC (from 740BC to well after 701BC). Jeremiah's predecessors in chronological order were: Amos, Hosea, Isaiah, Joel, Micah, Nahum, and Zephaniah. Zephaniah and Habakkuk were probably for a time his contemporaries, the first at the commencement, and the other near the end of his ministry.

It is important to familiarize ourselves with the historical background of any prophet, lest God sounds harsh. Therefore, **Read 2 Kings 21-25** as the historical background to Jeremiah's ministry.

What was the spiritual state of the nation that Josiah inherited (2 Kings 21:1-9, 16)? What was the most alarming sign (2 Kings 22:13 cf Deut 17:18, 31:11, 30: 15-18)? The Book of the Law was lost and people did not know it! God had commanded Moses that a copy of the Law should be kept not only reverently and carefully in the Temple, but also by the kings themselves and that the whole Law should be read to the people at their festivals. No wonder the king leading the people did much evil in God's sight, characterized by idol worship, children sacrifice (in the valley of the Son of Hinnom), sorcery and fortune-telling. But above all, what could have been a worse affront to God than defiling the place of worship with carved image, works of people's own hands, to displace God from His own house. Josiah's grandfather King Manasseh was a cruel oppressor of the weak (Jer 22:3,17) so that innocent blood flowed through all the streets of Jerusalem (2 Kings 21:16). **What was the consequence**

of these abominations committed by Manasseh (2 Kings 24: 3-4)? God sent Babylon to invade Judah which Jeremiah prophesied.

What was the significant event that happened in the 18th year of Josiah's reign (2 Kings 22: 8-13)? A copy of the Book of the Law was found in the house of the Lord by the high priest Hilkiah. By then Jeremiah had been prophesizing for four or five years. **What chain of events did it set off?** Josiah was a sincere servant of God. *If it had not been for the law, I would not have known sin* (Rom 7:7). The Law was like a mirror, exposing the sins in the land. He was mournful of the great sin they had committed to God when he heard the word of God read to him. He embarked on reforms to purge the worship of his people. With zeal he tried to restore a rule that manifested a fear of God. **How did the kings reign after Josiah (2 Kings 23:32&37, 24:9&19 cf 22:2)?** They did what was evil in God's sight like his fathers.

What can you conclude about Josiah's attempt to lead people to repentance and about the state of the people to whom Jeremiah ministered (2 Chron 36:12-16)? God gifted Josiah to the people, the rare pious and reforming king who did what was right in God's sight. They also witnessed the awful punishment of God on their brothers Israel, who were banished from their country by the Assyrians a century before. Given these favours, Judah was in an extremely corrupted state to pretend piety under Josiah and resume their abominable practices as soon as Josiah was taken from them by God. Their unfaithfulness to God was in a degree hardly credible. It defiled every moral principle and natural feeling. Yet the unfaithful people thought their ruin as prophesied by Jeremiah was impossible, holding God faithful to His covenant! This was the people whom Jeremiah was sent to minister to. His teaching encountered the hardness of hearts which were not tender for God's Word. We shall see what hard contest and pain he had to undergo during his life, earning him the nickname as "the weeping prophet".

How did Jeremiah's teaching compare with Isaiah's and other earlier prophets? While God had contended with the people by Isaiah and the other prophets, by Jeremiah and also by Ezekiel, God proved them guilty, and denounced on them the sentence of condemnation. Jeremiah was sent by God to proclaim to the people their last calamity – the horrific destruction of Jerusalem and their 70 year exile; it's all over with their earthly kingdom and the priesthood. Although Jeremiah also heralded God's grace and the salvation promised in Christ, he offered the people no hope of mercy until they had suffered the punishment due to their sins. His message was unpopular – who would like to hear judgement be pronounced on them?

II. The Prophet

Who was Jeremiah? How did he introduce himself? (V1) Jeremiah was of the priestly order. His father was not the high priest who found the book of the Law during Josiah's reign. He was from Anathoth which was in the territory of Benjamin, a few miles northeast to Jerusalem (Isaiah 10:26). [The priestly order should have been the nursery of the prophets. But when gross want of knowledge and ignorance prevailed among them, God chose his prophets from the other tribes, and thus exposed and condemned the priests. Isaiah was from the court, as he was of the royal family while Amos was a shepherd.]

When was he made a prophet (v6)? He was made a prophet when he was still very young. **How long was his ministry?** His public ministry spanned 40 years up to that point of Babylonian captivity. But he continued to prophesy after the destruction of Jerusalem (Chs. 40-44, 52) and we do not know for how long. Later on, we will see he was a reproving prophet, a weeping prophet and a suffering prophet.

4

III. His calling and office

How did Jeremiah explain his calling (v2 & 4) and what is the significance (2 Pet 1:19-21)? The word was given to him by God. The authority of prophets entirely belonged to God, and he must prove it. The office of prophets must be appointed by God and no one takes this honour to himself (Heb 5:4). **What did God do to Jeremiah in support of this office (v5)?** God predestined him to this office from before he was even formed. God appoints and sanctifies His people for their chosen roles. **What was the scope of his authority (v5)?** Although he was given as a prophet to his own people, his authority extended to heathen nations nearby.

Why was Jeremiah reluctant to take this call (v6)? Was he disobedient to God? No one according his own nature is fit for the work (2 Cor 3:5-6). The qualification for the office was brought forth not in Jeremiah but in God's election. His response was similar to that of Moses when he was first called. When he contemplated the calling, he felt he was wholly unequal to what the task demanded. He rightly felt acutely he was not sufficiently qualified, and would like to be excused. Such an arduous task on a youth, who could bear it? He thought there must be another better qualified and more courageous than he and therefore more suited for the task. What he had mistaken was that no one would be sufficiently qualified for the office if God did not make them so. The power is with God not with the person chosen. God will equip His servants for the assigned tasks. Anyone seeking to answer the challenge of the office in his own strength is doomed to fail – it is impossible and can't be done.

Was Jeremiah's concern justified? Why? He was a youth, implying that he was inexperienced and unskilled. Yet he had the right comprehension of the task: calling a hostile, proud and idolatrous corrupt people back to the truth of God and obedience was arduous if not impossible humanly speaking! No godly teacher can exercise his duty without being prepared for war.

How did God reassure Jeremiah (v7-8)? God directed Jeremiah to the doctrine that God's mission rested on God and not on the person sent. He was saying, "Look at me and don't look at yourself. Now do you have confidence?" Therefore, when God calls us, we ought to obey, however deficient we may be in all things: "Do not say, 'I am only a youth'; for to all to whom I send you, you shall go. Where you think you are deficient, I will provide." He also assured Jeremiah that He would protect him for his enemies were not greater than He. Jesus tells us that God the Father is greater than all (John 10:29). If we are still afraid and refuse to go, we are in effect scoffing God as less than our enemies. We are refuting God.

What does God's act in v9 symbolize (1 Pet 4:11)? It symbolizes that God's words were put in his mouth, which was consecrated for God's use. His authority comes from God Himself and his oracle was not to be disregarded or despised. It also means that God sealed his mouth from teaching his carnal wisdom as opposed to divine wisdom from above, based on his own presupposition and prejudices full of his opinions and ideas. **Who did he have authority over (v10)?** As such, he had authority over even kings, the highest authority in the land. In other words, <u>God ascribes here the highest authority to His own Word</u>. Should Jeremiah be afraid of anyone if he was armed with the power of the divine truth? Note that the authority does not rest with Jeremiah himself but God's word faithfully delivered by the prophet.

IV. <u>The message</u>

What was God's message to His people (v10)? God's message is made up of sound of thunders and sound of consolation, ruin and destruction before building and planting. **Why this order?**

As the Devil had erected his palace in the house of God, false religion had to be torn down and eradicated before He could build His temple. Their contempt for God and impiety was deep rooted. Indeed, all kinds of wickedness had prevailed everywhere as though the land had been filled with thorns and briers. Jeremiahs could not have planted or sown his heavenly doctrine until the land had been cleansed from so many vices and pollutions. Is 19:22 talks of striking before healing. We shall see this set of phrases repeated in the book like a theme or pattern.

> An almond tree is well known to flower even in winter, and in the coldest seasons. Therefore, it brings forth fruit earlier than other trees, and was said to "watch for spring".

What does the imagery of the almond tree tell about God's commitment to His Word and to Jeremiah His prophet (v11-12 cf Is 55:11)? It is impossible for God to lie (Heb 6:18). Here God underscores His Word with the power and might of His hand. His word will perform. **What are the implications?** (1) This is how we can tell true prophets from false prophets. True prophets who were sent by God and spoke His Word would have their prophecies come to pass for sure. (2) However, that power to accomplish what the prophets declared rests with God and not the prophets. (3) With that guarantee, God bids us to wait with quiet minds for the accomplishment of His Word.

What was the vision about Jerusalem in v13-15? Disaster would strike from the north. The Chaldeans from the north would come and invade them. They would be victorious that they would entirely rule and rest themselves as at their own homes, in the fields and before the city gates. **What does the boiling pot represent (v13)?** Many believe that it represents "the tribes of the kingdoms of the north". But Calvin interprets that the boiling pot refers to the nation of the Jews. It depicts God's judgement on her – to boil them until they were reduced to nothing. It was tilted to the north as it boiled on the side closest to the fire. More details will be filled out later but this is the sum of one half of Jeremiah's message – the sound of thunders. For this half, there was no hope of pardon. It was set in motion. **Who set this in motion (v15)?** Make no mistake, the Chaldeans came by the authority of God and not by chance or on their own accord. This is the difference between God's prophet and a historian. The former teaches us about God while the latter cannot. God directs all things by His sovereign power, and that nothing takes place except under His guidance and authority. **Why did God do this (v16) and why now and not before (Ps 51:4)?** They had committed great wickedness in forsaking Him, and many sins sprang out of that. God was silent before not because He did not know their sins, but it was judgement in reserve to give them time for repentance. But they abused His patience and kept sinning, ripening themselves for ruin. And now time was ripe for their disaster that would bring their kingdom and priesthood to an end, such that God is justified in His word and found blameless in His judgement. Glory is to Him as the equitable Judge. He always is; He does not have to prove it. It is so that we understand; it is for our education.

V17 literally reads "But you, gird up your loins". The Orientals wear long dresses, so the phrase means to prepare for work or action.

What did God foresee He was sending Jeremiah into (v19)? God knew He was sending Jeremiah into a crucible of great trials and opposition towards his ministry. He was to proclaim war in the name of God. Jeremiah's concerns were valid. **Who would be in opposition to him (v18)? Which group was most surprising to be on the list?** Jeremiah would be against the whole land, against the kings of Judah, its officials, its priests, and the people of the land. That the priests were against Jeremiah indicates the extent of corruption in the land and how lonely Jeremiah was to be. **How did God arm him for the war (v18, 19)?** God would have been unreasonable if He sent Jeremiah into the lion den with bare fists. God makes His servant invincible by promising that He will be his deliverer against his enemies, with the imagery of him being a fortified city. He would fight under God's protection with the imagery of an iron pillar and the bronze wall. Whatever he went through he would be victorious. **What four commands did God the Lord give Jeremiah (v17)?** (1) Get ready for work and action; (2) Arise; (3) Speak truthfully everything God has commanded him to speak, even the message that will offend and invite opposition; (4) "If you are timid, I will cause you really to fear before them." If with such promise of God he still lacks courage, then he is not worthy for God's protection and supply of strength.

Applications:

Christ redeems us from all lawlessness to purify for himself a people for his own possession who are zealous for good works (Titus 2:14).

Are we zealous or timid for good works which God has prepared in advance for us to do? Who is the Commander in Chief in your life?

Have you been struggling with any fears? How has God reassured you through the study?

SESSION TWO

Jeremiah 2-6

> Israel was a nation under King Saul, King David and King Solomon. After the death of Solomon, the nation split into two kingdoms in 922BC due to Solomon's sin (1 Kings 11:11-13, Ch. 12). The northern kingdom, made up of ten tribes, was called Israel. The southern kingdom, made up of Judah and Benjamin, was called Judah. The line of David continued in Judah. In 722BC, the northern kingdom was destroyed by Assyria due to their sin. This forms the backdrop to this text but especially 3:6-11. Israel was the faithless one and Judah was her treacherous sister.

I.   Israel's covenantal adultery and God's scandalous love
     (2:1-3:5)

What does God picture His covenantal relationship with Israel as (2:2)? What is the expectation in that relationship Israel did not fulfil (3:8)? God's relationship with His people is represented by a marital relationship. God binds Himself to Israel through the covenant, whereby He is the husband and Israel is the wife. In this relationship, the expectation is

10

<u>faithfulness</u> towards one another. When Israel broke the covenant, she was described as *faithless* and *a whore*. Being faithless means Israel committed spiritual *adultery* against her husband God when she ran to embrace false gods (2:28), greatly dishonouring God. God sent them away with *a decree of divorce* (3:8).

How would you construct an indictment against Israel based on chapter 2? Is God's fury justified?

(1) **God is a perfect husband.** How He brought her out of slavery, took care of her in the wilderness (v6) and planted her in a land of plenty flowing with milk and honey was the evidence (v7, 21). V5: *What wrong did your fathers find in me that they went far from me, and went after worthlessness, and became worthless?* His love for His bride cannot be faulted in any way.

(2) **Israel committed flagrant adultery.** Having experienced the wonderful and powerful redemption and God's extraordinary lovingkindness, their ingratitude was a heinous sin. The prophets prophesied by Baal (2:8). But lust cannot be restrained (2:24). She played the whore with many lovers (3:5). Her gods were as many as the cities (2:28) and she had gone after Baals (2:23). She was worse than the heathen nations covering the widest scope known, which would not change their gods even when they were no gods (2:10-11). Even the heathen nations demonstrated their loyalty towards their false gods, while Israel was treacherous against the one true God. As a consequence, she defiled the land and made God's heritage an abomination (2:7). They polluted worship and did what was abominable in God's sight. V23 (cf 7:31): *Look at your way in the valley; know what you have done.* In the Valley of the Hinnom, sons were burnt as an offering. They called a tree "their father" and a stone "their mother" (2:27). Her conduct shocked the heavens with great horror: *for my people have committed two evils: they have forsaken me, the fountain of living waters, and hewed out cisterns for themselves,*

broken cisterns that can hold no water (2:13). They turned their back to God and not their face (2:27). **What happened when people had not the fear of God in them (2:34, 6:6-7)?** Covenant infidelity necessarily results in ethical infidelity. The community degenerates into disorder, where oppression and violence is rampant.

(3) **God is long suffering.** Despite her appalling treatment of God, God does not give her up. He *still* contends with her and the children's children (2:9). He persistently sent prophets to warn them of their way and the impending judgement. They reminded the people of the law, called them to repent and pointed them back to God. **What did they do to the prophets (2:30)?** They killed them. They saw the prophets from God as against them because they told them what they did not want to hear. 2:14: **Is Israel a slave? Is he a homeborn servant? Why then has he become a prey? (2:19)** God had adopted them as His people, and had promised to be bountiful to them as to render them in every way happy. Indeed, why then did they lose their freedom and become miserable? It was their sin that rendered them miserable. They became a prey to their professed enemies because sin deprived them of God's protection. **What was God's intention (2:30)?** Correction.

(4) **Israel was obstinate in their rebellion. Did they respond to correction (2:30, 5:3)?** No. They had made their face harder than rock; they refused to repent. **What was their response when they faced trouble (2:18)?** They sought external help rather than God. And they were not reflecting on their wrongdoings. **Did they show any remorse (2:35, 2:22, 2:26 cf 3:3, 3:4-5, 4:4)?** They pleaded not guilty. They thought that the cleansing rituals made them clean but God denied that it was working. They defiled the ceremonial law as a licence to sin, contrary to God's intention of the law. Their stain of guilt remained before God despite their religion. Israel should be ashamed but they were not. They

sinned egregiously and did not even blush. They refused to be ashamed (3:3). They might be circumcised but not their hearts (4:4). **What had they become as a result of sin (2:5, 8)?** Worthless and unprofitable. **What made Israel's case so hopeless (2:8, 26-27 cf 5:4-5)?** The rot was right through to the top. Those who should have instructed the people in the knowledge of God took no care to get the knowledge of Him themselves. Those who were supposed to set an example in their leadership had departed from true worship themselves.

(5) **What was God's verdict on them (3:5)?** *Behold, you have spoken, but you have done all the evil that you could.* **Both heathens and Israel committed idolatry. What made Israel's transgression worse (2:19)?** They committed apostasy or backsliding (NIV). They had tasted God's goodness in abundance, received instructions and favour. They appeared devoted to God but lived as a whore, a capital offence to the holy God. Their profession aggravated their crime. God's lovingkindness and faithfulness has made Israel's treachery inexcusable. They were condemned justly.

Applications:

Does God need our approval of His wrath against His people? If not, then why is God bothered to lay it plain to us at such great length? It is to prepare our hearts for salvation, to know what we are saved from. Yet salvation is not the end. What are we saved to? To worship God. It is for His glory that He is a just and holy God. He goes into great length to make His justice known to us so that (1) we admire and praise Him intelligently, (2) we have confidence in His justice even when we don't understand, and (3) we know ourselves better about our innate sense of justice as we are made in His image.

What are the lessons on sin we can learn? (1) The cause of sin is our forgetting God, forsaking God, turning our back on God and having no fear of God in us (5:24). In other words, the root of sin is idolatry, which is strangely intoxicating. Remembering God, meditating His Word and deeds is a great antidote to that, as His Word has instructed. As ladies, we should be very convicted by 2:32 that we think about our clothes and accessories more than God – *Can a virgin forget her ornaments, or a bride her attire? Yet my people have forgotten me days without number.* (2) Apostasy makes sins worse. (3) Sin is an evil thing in its nature. We can become very skilled in sinning – *they are 'wise'* – *in doing evil! But how to do good they know not* (4:22). On the road of repentance, it is crucial that we recognise sin as shame. Shamelessness is pernicious (6:15). It is Satan's way to pacify our guilt. *Only acknowledge your guilt, that you rebelled against the LORD your God...* (3:13). (4) Infidelity to God and promiscuity go hand in hand. It is unlikely that we will stay with one false god but have "many lovers" and "many gods", gods without number. Why? Once we transgress the set boundary, effectively we have no limits. Besides, false gods do not satisfy. Are we surprised by the appeal of polytheism? (5) We excel in finding all excuses to defend ourselves and plead not guilty (2:35). (6) Sin brings us misery. *Know and see that it is evil and bitter* (2:19). The bitterness of Judah's sin will be unfolded.

What is the biggest lie of Satan (Gen 3:4, Jer 2:35, 6:14)? The biggest lie and delusion of all is that we can sin with impunity, that God will not judge us or punish us, that we surely will not die. We call Him bad names when He does punish us. We are convinced of peace when we should be disturbed and restless. Satan's scheme has been very effective from Day one with Eve. He is very successful in blinding us with the extreme myopia to this life that we can't picture eternity. He also trivialises hell as if it were a joke and people do not mind dressing up like devils. Hell is portrayed as heaven for the rebellious. It dulls people's conscience that they are in need of salvation. At best people procrastinate if they have not rejected the notion as outright irrelevant. God helps us.

God's love for us is scandalous. Why (3:1, 22)? We deserve to be thrown out many times over but God asks us to return! God offers what we human could not have accepted if we were in the husband's shoes. Yet we are sinners while God is holy, who has borne much worse dishonour than we could ever have because His name is infinitely higher than ours. He never gives up on us, His remnant (4:27, 5:10). This shows the depth of God's love for the undeserving sinners which no words can capture adequately. It should overwhelm us, stir our hearts and leave us speechless. If it doesn't, we should meditate upon it until it does, followed by an outburst of praise and thanksgiving for His scandalous love is our only hope to our wretchedness.

II.   God's renewed call to repentance (3:6-4:4)

How did God establish that *Faithless Israel has shown herself more righteous than treacherous Judah* **(3:11)?** Judah had two advantages over Israel that made their impenitence much more inexcusable. (1) Seeing the fall of Israel, Judah did not take heed the warning at all about her spiritual adultery with stone and tree, just like her faithless sister. She did not return to God with their whole heart (3:10). (2) This was worse also because God gave Judah a good king Josiah. He instigated widespread reforms to return the people to true worship. **What was God's verdict on the effort 3:10?** They returned in pretence and God hates hypocrisy. God took Josiah away from them to hasten their demise. God was proven right in His judgement as they reverted back to abominable practices once Josiah was gone.

3:12-4:2 is a call to repentance. To whom was it directed? "Towards the north" means Israel – the nation already obliterated and people scattered and banished from the land. **What is the gist of the message (cf Ps 30: 5)?** Remember God is teaching us about Himself all the time. Here we see God is merciful. We have seen that justice means that God has every right to annihilate us but *His anger is but for a moment and His favour is for a lifetime* (Ps 30:5). If people hold a lifetime grudge against God's momentary anger, that God in our mind is a misrepresentation because we ignore His lifetime of mercy. **God's anger had already fallen on Israel. In what sense was He merciful?** Their sins had been punished and God is not irreconcilable. The punishment was not such that all hope of deliverance was stamped out. God asks them to return and there will be healing for their faithlessness (v22). **How?** By his pardoning mercy and renewing grace.

What do God-sent shepherds feed their flock (3:15)? In contrast to the bad shepherds that Israel and Judah had, God-sent shepherds are after God's own heart and feed the sheep with knowledge and understanding. It starts with their own faith walk. **Where do they get the knowledge and understanding from?** Shepherds are necessarily men of God's Word, both to know God's heart for themselves and to impart knowledge and understanding to those entrusted to them. This is what we should expect from our shepherds. This points us to Christ as our perfect Shepherd in John 10.

What is the gospel message (3:12-18)? The gospel message has always been that if the people return to Him, they would obtain forgiveness of sins. But be sure that this is not a trade and this is not justice. God of His free will issues this offer to us and ties Himself to His promise that He will be merciful to us, that He will remember our sins no more. That repentance procures forgiveness is grounded in Christ's atonement work for sinners. Mindful that we don't take His mercy as our right. **Is there a place for the ark of covenant?** The ark of covenant was the focal point of OT worship. It represented the presence of God. It was also called the mercy seat, where God met with His people. The division between Israel and Judah ran deep. Israel had the number and the riches, the temporal advantages but Judah had the temple and the ark, a spiritual superiority which became Judah's pride to their hurt. The prophecy foretells that the ark and all the ceremonial law would be fulfilled in Christ, the mercy seat where reconciliation between sinners and God would take place. The ark of the covenant of the Lord, which once was such a prized property, *shall not come to mind or be remembered or missed* and *shall not be made again* because it has been bettered! The shadow has no place when the reality is here. Judah and Israel will be united in harmony, foretelling that God's people will be gathered from all nations (v17). **Where will they be gathered to (v17)?** Jerusalem, not the earthly one but the heavenly Jerusalem where is the throne and habitation of the eternal God.

Identify the elements of true repentance (3:13, 17, 24-25; 4:1). We must acknowledge our guilt for our obstinate rebellion against God (v13). We need to turn away from stubbornly following our evil hearts (v17). We come to our senses to see sin as shame and dishonour, rather than pride and honour, and that sin is destructive leading to consequences of death and ruin (v24). True repentance produces action in *removing detestable things from God's presence and do not waver* (4:1). Jeremiah is bidding Israelites to return to God with sincerity and not hypocrisy. It is not an outward circumcision but an inward circumcision of the heart (4:4).

III. Prediction of Judah's fate 4:3-31

Turning to Judah, what did Jeremiah ask Judah to do in 4:3-4? He asked them to prepare the ground to receive God's mercy with an inner contrition, or disaster would strike them. They would share the fate of her sister, Israel. **Were they circumcised to listen (6:10)?** No, they did not listen. They had become worthless like their worthless idols (5:21). **What was the difference of judgement this time from previously?** Lesser

17

calamities had not shaken the Jews from their pride in spiritual superiority. God's wrath was ready to punish sins (4:4b) in destruction; it was unquenchable.

What was the punishment predicted (4:5-18)? God sent forth a mighty enemy *from the north* (v6) to attack Jerusalem (its prowess, strong and swift, depicted graphically). The destruction would be sudden (6:26), and their attacker would be cruel and merciless (6:23). Those in power were discouraged (v9) and the end result bitter (v18). Destruction and desolation was to be expected (v7) and mourning would be the right response (v8). **Who to blame (v18)?** *Your ways and your deed have brought this upon you.* **Did Jeremiah agree (v22)?** May we not be foolish and have no understanding, only "wise" in doing evil and have no idea of how to do good. **How did God reply to that (v30 cf 6:19-20)?** They made themselves appear better than they were, by vainly beautifying themselves in the eyes of the world at the price of looking deformed in God's sight in false worship. They deceived others as well as themselves. They were unprepared for the truth when their grotesqueness came to light and the affliction would be felt doubly hard.

In 4:19-26, Jeremiah lamented his watchman's grief, which God lays it plain in 6:17! Like Jesus, he was a man of sorrow. Ponder on that.

What did he liken the desolation to in 4:23-26 (cf Gen 1:2)? It is creation undone! The land was out of order and in confusion. **This is sound of thunders. Why must the nation be plucked up?** To teach them horror of sins and to purge their idolatry. **Despite severe punishment, what is the sound of consolation (v27)?** The ruin of Judah as a nation is not the full end. God punishes severely but He would never cast off His covenant people. The character of God's rebuke of His people is such that sound of thunder is always mixed with sound of consolation, destruction is for a purpose of healing and restoration.

God always warns before He wounds, not just through Jeremiah here but in the law as well (Deut 28:15ff). He is doing nothing unexpected.

IV. Judah's response and God's judgement affirmed (Ch. 5-6)

How did Judah respond (5:3, 12-13)? They refused to believe that God would judge them, not least because they held Jerusalem. They understood God as being faithful to the covenant, which they interpreted as judgement would not fall on them. They had not learnt the lesson of Israel. **Whom did they believe (5:30-31)?** False prophets could deceive and cause havoc because people love to hear them! **What did their stubborn rebellion prompt God to do (6:30)?** Reject them. **Who was God punishing, individuals or the nation (v9)?** The fact is that the consequences of national sins are borne by the godly as well as the ungodly. We see Jeremiah, Daniel and Ezekiel afflicted due to the nation's sin. This is God's grace to the ungodly as the impact must have been softened by having godly people among them. The day will come when the ungodly faces their fate alone and in eternity. **What was the logic in God's chosen form of punishment (5:19)?** God returns their way upon their heads (Eze 22:31). As they loved to serve foreign gods in God's land, God banished them to the foreign land to serve strangers. **Amid judgement, note the sound of consolation in emphasis (v10, v18).** Even in those days, God will not make a full end of them.

Finally, if we feel unsettled with the prophecy of impending predicaments, where does God point us to (6:16)? The good way lies in the ancient paths. The highway to God is ancient because God is never changed, so is His way. He is called the Ancient of Days. It has always been the same way, well-trodden and in turn well-proven by past saints before us. Amid the calamities and chaos, we have the oasis in this verse which guides us on a path to rest for our soul. I know the Futurist and the Progressive tells us otherwise like, "The human value system

... must be updated and changed through education and thought-out introspection...[and] the environment surrounding that value system must change to support the new worldview" (From One or Two, by Peter Jones, Loc149). Remember the Bible tells us the opposite.

Questions for personal reflection:

Are you wholly God's or do you entertain a secret lover in your heart? Is there anything more important to you than God?

Do you *remember* or *forget* God for most of the time? Whose counsel do you listen to, God's or others'? Spiritually, do we vainly beautify ourselves to appear better than we are?

Confess to God any convictions that the study has brought to light.

Give thanks for His scandalous love. Prepare your heart anew to receive His boundless mercy.

SESSION THREE

Jeremiah 7-10

I.   Taking down Judah's pride (7:1-29)

TEMPLE: God created the Garden of Eden as His sanctuary to dwell with His people (Gen 2:4-17). After He brought Israel out of Egypt, He instructed them to build the tabernacle for Him to live among His people (Ex 25:1-9). King Solomon built the temple as a more permanent place for God to dwell with His people in the Promised Land (1 Kings 7-8). These structures points forward to the true temple, Jesus Christ (John 1:14; 2:21). All who are united to Him by faith are being built into a temple for God's Spirit to indwell (Eph. 2:19-22; 1 Pet 2:4-8).

(Quoted from *Knowing the Bible: Jeremiah,* by Matthew Harmon, 2016, Crossway, p.11)

At the start of Ch. 7, God assigned Jeremiah to an arduous task. What was it (7:1-4)? God sent Jeremiah to stand at the temple gate to proclaim to <u>all</u> men of Judah who entered the house to worship God that their supreme sense of security in the Temple of God was misplaced; they had believed deceptive words. To have all men of Judah gathered at the Temple suggests that it was likely to be a feast day. Population of Jerusalem typically swelled during those times. Where else was more inflammable to preach this message than at the temple gate to the self-righteous crowd who would be most hostile to the message? This was God's Word very publicly proclaimed as if at the rooftop for the maximum impact. **Would that setting be our natural choice? Explain.** We generally do not like confrontation and this could be a hindrance. Those who do not think they need to hear the gospel are those who need to hear it most. The Gospel is confrontational. God shoots directly at the heart of our problem without apology. God's prophet must not fear the face of men or he cannot be faithful to God. A lamp certainly is not to be put under the table. This applies to us as well.

What falsehood had they believed in the Temple of God (Deut 29:17-19 esp v19)? The good gifts of God turn sour if they replace God Himself in our hearts. The Temple of God was the pinnacle of Judah's pride, representing God's dwelling among them. They believed the Temple of the Lord as if a foolproof talisman that guaranteed their protection, honour and blessings, as if to say, "We have the Temple in our midst, what could go wrong with us?" The Temple became their shelter and refuge and not God. (Later on, we see that God accuses them of not knowing Him.) <u>Extraordinary privileges can become our curse if we put our confidence in them instead of God</u>. **What showed that their worship at the Temple was false worship (7:8-11 cf Is 29:13, Mark 11:15-19)?** There can be no true worship without a life of obedience! Coming to the Temple while breaking every commandment, especially going after false gods, is an abomination and great dishonour to God. His displeasure was physically expressed when Jesus cleansed the temple in anger, charging the false worshippers as turning His Father's house into a den of robbers, echoing v11 here. **What functions does false worship do to the people?** (1) A cultivated appearance of goodness and righteousness by being religious blinds the world to our true colours, so that we don't invite censure. (2) We employ it to stop the mouth of our conscience so that we may go easy on ourselves to keep sinning. We are effectively deceiving others as well as ourselves. Arguably this is the worst of sin when God's sacred things are made into a licence to sin. **Application: What can we draw to examine our own worship life?** This is a great warning to us. Worship is not confined to an hour and a half worship service on Sundays but our whole life. We need to examine ourselves if our worship is backed up by a life of obedience to God or it only provokes God's displeasure. Make sure we don't do churchianity (man-centred religious services, *City Lives*, p. 152) but Christianity. **How was their civic life (7: 5-7)?** "You cannot deviate from truth without, in some measure, deviating from practical righteousness" (Spurgeon, *Words of Counsel to the leaders*, p.117). We see widespread injustice and oppression and violence towards the powerless and vulnerable. These were the ways and deeds that the prophet was highlighting and urged them to amend.

What happened when Jeremiah's prophecy of destruction to Jerusalem and the Temple met with this false belief? Jeremiah was not believed. They believed that the sacred Temple would protect them even from God's judgement: How could God destroy the Temple, especially when He must be faithful to His covenant promise of the everlasting line and kingdom of David? **God shattered this false belief by reminding them of the precedent in what He did to Shiloh (7:12-15). What happened to Shiloh (see Josh 18:1, 1 Sam 4:22, Ps 78:60-61)?** God set up the tabernacle at Shiloh when Israel first took possession of Canaan, i.e. before David made Jerusalem the capital. God forsook His dwelling there and it became a monument of divine vengeance of their wickedness. Just as the glory departed from Shiloh when the ark was captured by the Philistines, God told them that their confidence in "the Temple of the Lord" was badly misplaced; Shiloh represented a precedent to Jerusalem's doom. When God's glory departed, the city would not be protected. **How were the people tempting this terrible fate (7:13, 25)?** They persistently (or *again and again* in NIV) did not listen to God's prophets.

What was the significance when God asked Jeremiah not to pray for Judah (7:16 cf 7:29)? It shows that the decree was set; His wrath ready to be poured out was unquenchable (v20). God asked Jeremiah not to pray for the withholding of this judgement because it would be against God's will and would not be granted positively. But we never stop praying for the salvation of people's souls. **What is the difference between the unquenchable fire here (7:20) and hell (Ps 30:5)?** It is a foretaste of hell and we should be terrified. God's judgement on earth still demonstrates His mercy in that it will pass after a brief time, while hell is for eternity without respite – just imagine that. Too long a period of peacetime, we may have lost grip of what hell is like. Many today trivialise hell and lose the sense of urgency. I believe repeated calamities in history with scenes of devastation and atrocities and sea of suffering serve to inject realism into our comprehension of the misery of hell. Compared to history books and film documentaries, the Bible descriptions are tamed and gracious. Because we easily forget, calamities come back in cycles.

What is God's only quarrel with Judah (7:18, 21-24 cf 1 Sam 15:22)? Their disobedience. Obedience is better than sacrifices. Their idol worship was very personally involved (v18). With their stiff neck, sacrifices became a bribe to purchase a licence to sin. His people behaved as though they could dictate the terms of how they approached God and God of course would tolerate none of it. He reminded the people that the covenant is not about sacrifices but a relationship – that He will be our God and we shall be His people. **Why did God send Jeremiah to proclaim His word when He knew the people would not listen (7:27-28)?** To bring their evil hearts to light and out in the open, so that we know God's Word is justified.

II.   Hell fire on the loose (7:30-8:3)

What is this place reference *Topheth* (Is 30:31-33)? In the context of Isaiah, Topheth means the burning place, which had been prepared to bury the dead bodies of the Assyrian besiegers when God was still fighting for Israel. **What was the valley used for in Jeremiah's time?** For children sacrifice which God abhorred. **What would take place at Topheth? How were dead bodies treated?** The destruction of Jerusalem would be terrible. Topheth would be the dumping place for dead bodies from the city. So high would be the causalities that *there was no more room elsewhere* (v32), and there were no one to bury the dead. It would be called the Valley of Slaughter. There was so much horror and suffering that it was no surprise the voice of gladness and mirth was silenced in the city. Evil pursues sinners even after death. While the slain were denied a decent burial for human dignity, the wicked from the previous generations would not escape through their death but met the same infamous end as their counterparts with their bones exhumed from their graves and scattered. It foreshadows that on the last day, the living and the dead will be raised to judgement. **How was the horror and misery described (8:3)?** Death is preferred to life, in an utter despair of this life. Is this not a description for hell? **What was the scene set for (Eze 37)?** The scene was set for Ezekiel's prophecy on the resurrection power of the gospel. God showed Ezekiel of a valley full of very dry bones that could not possibly have any life in them. Nor could they revive themselves. Ezekiel was instructed to prophesy over these dry bones that God will breathe on these slain, that they may live (Eze 37:9). God said to Ezekiel: *Son of man, these bones are the whole house of Israel. Behold, they say, 'Our bones are dried up, and our hope is lost; we are indeed cut off.'...And you shall know that I am the LORD, when I open your graves, and raise you from your graves, O my people. And I will put my Spirit within you, and you shall live, and I will place you in your own land.* (v11, 13-14). **What was the infamous valley for in NT time (cf Mark 9:47)?** It was a rubbish incinerator just outside Jerusalem where "their worm does not die and the fire is not quenched" (Mark 9:47) with a constant stench. Interestingly the word translated as "hell" in the gospels is *Gehenna* referring to this rubbish dump. Hebrew is a very visual language; it means that the people were very visual in their thinking. To the Jews, the history of this valley epitomises what hell is. It is clear that God is giving us a picture of hell and we should take heed.

III. Backwards not forwards (8:4-17)

This section elaborates on 7:24: *But they did not obey or incline their ear, but walked in their own counsels and the stubbornness of their evil hearts, and went backwards and not forwards.* If they had begun well, they went backwards (to Egypt, the land of slavery) and did not go forwards into the liberty that God had delivered them. **How did God describe His people's ways (8:5-7)?** God accused them of *perpetual backsliding* (ESV) which NIV prosaically translates as *always turned* away. They showed no signs of repentance but would have their own way. They were like a horse eagerly rushing into the battle, scorning any restraints but running headlong to the instruments of death and slaughter (v6).   Even wildlife intrinsically understands God's rules and providence for them, but His people knew not the rules of God, making them worse than the beasts (v7).

What was the extent of this corruption (8:8, 10)? It permeated through all the layers of the society from the least to the greatest with greediness and falsehood. However, the elites were more responsible as the impact of their evil and lies was magnified through the power levers they controlled. **What is the impact of false teaching (8:11,15)?** The false prophets and the priests lie to the people and patch them up lightly. They say to them that they are good to go when they are not; that there is "peace, peace" where there is no peace. That reassurance works like a spell that dulls their senses towards their danger. Their unpreparedness and disappointment only aggravates the impact of the affliction on them. God confirms that riders are ready for their destruction (v16-17).

IV. Jeremiah's lamentation (8:19-9:26)

What was the nature of Jeremiah's grief (8:18-21, 9:1)? Here we meet our weeping prophet! A watchman's grief is deep because of his macro vision of the calamities ahead that he feels absolutely helpless in stopping. It was deepened further for Jeremiah as God had commanded him not to pray for its reversal on behalf of the people (7:16). It was a grief as lonely as his voice that fell on deaf ears. The grief was not personal but concerned the fate of the nation. We may be chuffed when we are proved right but not for a watchman who grieves rather than rejoices in being proved right. "The miseries of our country ought to be very much the grief of our souls. A gracious spirit will be a public spirit, a tender spirit, a mourning spirit" (Matthew Henry's commentary). **Application: do we have this gracious spirit to mourn for the state of our nation or even the world and the Church? Reflect.**

What was the content of his grief (8:22 cf Eze 18: 23, 32)? It was not that there was no balm or physician but that the people would not admit the application or submit to the methods of cure. It is like a patient who refuses to give up a habit that will kill him. This is the same grief when sinners reject the gospel or perpetual backsliders reject God's correction. We mourn deeply. Similarly, has God *any pleasure in the death of the wicked and not rather that he should turn from his way and live?* God answers, *for I have no pleasure in the death of anyone… so turn, and live* (Eze 18:23, 32). **What does it say about God's servant?** We cannot go and tell the gospel to people unfeelingly. We tell it from our hearts and experience that hurt of love. God moves us with a compassion for people, which is impossible to sustain if not from Christ. The impact of God's Word is having our hearts enlarged as we are aligned to His concerns and care more and more beyond our personal life.

At the personal level, did Jeremiah enjoy his situation and why (9:2-6 cf 2 Pet 2:7-8, Ps 119:136)? The sorrow was hard to bear because it seemed hopeless at the personal level; there was nothing he could do to make the people change their path. Furthermore, these were the people who grieved him, hated him and abused him. The company of treacherous and lying people who do not fear God is no delight to godly people (v2). *My eyes shed streams of tears, because people do not keep your law* (Ps 119:136). Godliness naturally repels ungodliness, and truth stands to oppose falsehood. Treachery and falsehood are such that you can't trust anyone even those closest to you like your brother and neighbour. If you love God, people who refuse to know God intimately (v6) is also heart-breaking. [NB: NIV translates it as *refuse to acknowledge God* which is different meaning.] The lawless deeds around him torment the soul of the righteous. In his desperation, Jeremiah fantasized that going to the desert and leaving them would be a relief (v2). **Application: If a godly man feels this way about living among spiritually filthy company, imagine what it was like for God-incarnate! What condescension!! Marvel at it.**

What is God's reply (9:7-9)? Why (Is 26:9-10)? Their ruin was marked and God could do nothing else. NB: He punishes not individuals but the nation collectively, which is "uncircumcised in heart (9:26)" in God's sight. We carry our national sins. God's judgement teaches the world righteousness. In contrast if God shows favour to the wicked, people won't learn righteousness and won't see the majesty of God (Is 26: 9-10). **What God would do in judgement (9:12-16) is told in His Law (Deut 29:18).**

Why does God appeal to the women in 9:20? They are more apt to absorb and understand grief and fear. They are likely to get it before the men. **What is our instinctive response in face of adversities (9:23-24)?** We turn to our strengths – wisdom, wealth and might – to fix it. But God says we will find these fail us when they are most needed. Our only boast is in understanding and knowing Him as who He really is. This leads us to

V. The folly of idolatry (ch. 10)

How does God expose the folly of idolatry (see also Rom 1:25)? Paul says there are only two possible kinds of worship: of the creation or of the Creator. The maker of anything must be superior to the things made. So why would we worship something that is made and crafted by our own hands except that our hearts are blinded by delusion and we have lost our mind? Our stupidity in worshipping scarecrows as idols is even more glaring against who the one true God is: the living and Sovereign God of all creation with unsurpassed wisdom, power and might, commanding an authority that He speaks and it is so. Here shows that an understanding of the Creation commands the pivotal position as "the head of divine philosophy" (*Creation and Change*, by Douglas Kelly, 1997, Mentor, p.16).

What is the difference in Jeremiah's lamentation in 10:19-25 compared with the section above? The tone has changed from being sullen to a gracious submission to God's will; he was at peace with it. It is teaching us the right attitude in receiving calamities from God's hand, that we will bear it graciously, trusting in God's wisdom and His grace that will make it work for our good in the end. **What is our prayer in the situation (10:24 cf Ps 6:1)?** That God does not discipline us in His wrath but in His love for no one can bear His full wrath which would mean utter annihilation.

Questions for reflection:

Is church to you like "the Temple of the Lord" to the Jews?

What does worship mean to you: your whole life or only Sunday service? Are there any areas of your life that "do not know the rule of God"?

Contemplate the concrete notion of hell and what Christ has borne in our stead on the Cross. Let this better understanding of what we have been saved from fill us with fuller joy and in turn drive us to praise God more exuberantly for the Trinitarian work in our redemption.

SESSION FOUR

Jeremiah 11-13

In this session, watch how God as the Father handles His rebellious children (the Jews) on the one hand and movingly counsels Jeremiah's troubled heart for his spiritual growth on the other.

I.   Sin exposed and God's wrath (11:1-17)

> Covenant: a binding agreement between two parties, typically involving a formal statement of their relationship, a list of stipulations and obligations for both parties, a list of witnesses to the agreement, and a list of curses for unfaithfulness and blessings for faithfulness to the agreement.
>
> (Quoted from *Knowing the Bible: Jeremiah*, by Matthew Harmon, 2016, Crossway, p.11)

God uses the (Old) Covenant to teach His people about their sins (see also Rom 7:7). How? There are nuances to the general term "sin" in the OT. The covenant here refers to the Law. (See 31:32 and Calvin, *Institutes* 3:11:10.) It shows up our *sin* as coming short or failing to hit the target. It defines our *transgressions* as violating God's Law wilfully in impudent disobedience. It makes our *iniquities* surface, which are faults in our character, crookedness in our nature, which bend God's Law to serve us, to make us look right, to hide our deeds and deceive others. We see the Law displays Judah's hypocrisy, which God heavily criticised through Jeremiah. This hypocrisy only got more sophisticated down the generations and epitomised in the Jewish religious practice led by the Pharisees in Jesus' days. As God confronted Judah here, Jesus similarly confronted the whole religious system of the Jews cumulating in His pronouncing judgement on the Temple which would be destroyed again in AD70 with Jerusalem (Matthew 21:18-22).

What are the terms of the covenant (11:1-8 cf Lev 26:11-13)? God's ultimate desire is to tabernacle and walk among His people. The goal of the covenant is to purify a people for His own treasured possession, "so shall you be my people, and I will be your God", so shall God be able to tabernacle among His people without His soul abhorring them. To accomplish this goal, God needs His people to incline their ears and obey His voice. The goal of the covenant is never changed.

What is the *conspiracy* God refers to and who are the conspirators in 11:9? God does not see sinning as a private personal matter but a conspiracy implying a collective action of the conspirators. They were the men of Judah and the inhabitants of Jerusalem and across the generations (as they copied and expanded on what their forefathers did) conspiring to overthrow God's kingdom with their inventions, pretension and sophistication to cause confusion with their numerous counterfeits.

We see parallels here with 7:21-29 and later in Chs. 18 &19. Why does God keep repeating Himself? It shows (1) His patience with His children; (2) the consistency in His instruction; and (3) on doctrinal truth, no compromise to accommodate the children's wayward behaviour. If even God has to repeat Himself persistently to His stiff necked children, we shouldn't be surprised we have to too with ours!

Why do false gods tend to multiply (11:13)? There is only one truth against many errors. If people tell you there are many truths which co-exist, we should be alarmed. If I have my truth and you have yours, it means that we have as many truths as there are number of people! In our days of postmodernism, the only truth allowed is that there is no truth! This is a conspiracy against God. **Application: Beware that we don't unwittingly become conspirators by connivance.**

How does God express His wrath (11:11, 14-17)? The people cannot flee from justice. Disaster will strike and privileges will be withheld. In this sense, every sin against God is a sin against ourselves. Cutting off prayer is listed as a threat or punishment. Prayer is a great privilege God's people enjoy.

Application: Do we inadvertently forfeit a great privilege by our prayerlessness? Reflect.

II.   Jeremiah wrestled with difficulties (11:18-12:17)

God revealed to Jeremiah a plot against him by men of his hometown (11:18-21). What was it? People of his hometown Anathoth (v1) threatened to kill him if he prophesies in the name of God (v19, 21). **What does 11:19 remind you of (see Is 53:7)?** A description of Christ. We should not be surprised that we share Christ's suffering. He explains that a servant is not greater than his master. If Christ was persecuted, so shall His disciples (John 15:20, Matt 10:24-25). **What does it convey about Jeremiah's emotions?** He felt wronged, maybe even betrayed, by his kinsmen, people who should best love, support and understand him. *But I was like a gentle lamb led to the slaughter. I do not know it was against me they devised schemes* (v19). **God will avenge the godly. How do you understand imprecatory prayer on your enemies (11:20)?** Jeremiah is not asking God for a personal revenge on his enemies but for His justice which the wicked seek to suppress. Jeremiah is subscribing to God's will and not prescribing what He should do.

When we have things we don't understand, how should we approach God (12:1-4)? We are allowed to wrestle and reason with God, but we must approach it with an attitude of learning and not contending. *Your righteousness is like the mountains of God; your judgements are like the great deep; man and beast you save, O LORD* (Ps 36:6). We must abide in what we know as true that *righteous is He* (v1) before we set out on our inquiry.

In 12:1-4, Jeremiah was agitated about God's tardiness in judgement of the wicked who had enjoyed prosperity, and the creation was groaning (see also 12:10-11). **What is the lesson for Jeremiah to learn (12:5-6)?** Lesser calamities are rehearsals for the real challenge ahead. They are training provided for the godly to face the big moments that God has called them to in life. *If you are wearied racing with men on foot, how are you to compete with horses?* (v5) **Application: how are we running our race? Are we having a good workout of faith and grace? Are we faithful over a little that we may be entrusted over much (Matt 25:21)? Reflect.**

God's judgement starts with 12:7. What is it? What are the consequences (12:7-13)? God's glory left His temple, and His protection and blessing retreat. The people become preys and the land is made desolate. Destroyers are coming with their swords and "no flesh has peace" exposing the false prophets. The curse of futility rules (12:13) (more later).

Amid the horror of judgement, where is mercy (12:14-17)? *Pluck up* means to draw up the roots and by force. God promise He will pluck up Judah's evil neighbours. Though the Jews have sinned, yet these are not their judges; nor have they any right to punish them for their unfaithfulness. It has been God's will to choose them for His heritage. Therefore, in the prophecies, not only judgement on God's people is spelt out but also judgement on their enemies sent to execute God's judgement on His people. God also promise that He will use to the same force to draw back His own from the cruelty of these nations. God always reserves a remnant so that the covenant is not void. The deliverance of His elect takes a great deal of effort too as these captors will not easily let His people go. But their opposition will not foil God's plan. To His remnants is compassion, which is extended to the heathens, bearing the gospel light here. Even though they taught His people to swear by Baal, as long as they diligently learn the ways of His people and swear by His name, God will build them up in the midst of His people (v16). For those who will not listen, God will pluck up and destroy (v17).

III.   External symbols and Jeremiah's heartache (Ch. 13)

Why does God teach with metaphors? What does it say about our daily life? To the spiritually dull minded people, it is easier for a spiritual lesson to strike home with an external symbol from their familiarity. Put it differently God has weaved His truth into His creation as His visual aids ready to be used to teach us spiritual lessons. This is an infinite stock for us to discover and utilise for our creativity!

What is God's sharp message to the Jews about the "ruined loincloth" (13:1-11)? What is the heart of the problem with the Jews (v9 cf v15, 17)? Great pride needs to be humbled. The worthiness of the Jews stemmed from God uniting them to Him and they knew it. They gloried proudly in the thought that God was bound to them. That would have been true if they had not insulted and dishonoured His name by running after false gods. God showed them that their dignity had indeed been great but He would mar it, and in so doing, smash their false confidence with which they deceived themselves. Casting them out into exile for *many days* and seeing their glory rot in base condition aimed to shake them to their core. God's lesson is sharp and painful but it is instructive and corrective to the very point, showing His wisdom, if only the Jews would not refuse correction. **Where is the loincloth hidden (v4)?** The Euphrates, the river of Babylon. **How many will be taken into exile (v19)?** All Judah is taken into exile, wholly taken into exile.

What is the second metaphor teaching about the condition of the Jews (13:12-14 cf Rev 17:1-2, 18:3)? Life away from God is like drunkenness, intoxication of alcohol. This is a picture of God giving us up, and let us be filled with our own evils and calamities. **How would you describe drunkenness?** Soundness of mind and reason are lost but in its stead are confusion and incoherence. We stagger on our feet. We are emboldened, unaware of danger. With inhibitions lifted, we are reckless and loud in our sins and know no shame. We are drowned in fake merriment so that we are oblivious of our brokenness. Above all, how often does drunkenness lead us to dash against one another? Drunkenness is harmful to ourselves. **Application: Is our nation filled with drunkenness? Reflect.**

Why is Jeremiah moved to tears while the people are unmoved (v17 cf Ecc 1:18)? Jeremiah has clear spiritual sight and he knows that the prophecy is certainty. Therefore he knows better than anyone the terrors that await his kinsmen; he knows how much their obstinacy will cost them. His public preaching is mingled with tears. Preacher of God cannot preach with a cold heart and

<u>pure intellect</u>. **Application: do we have this compassion for the lost?**

The king in v18 refers to King Jehoiakim. God's message does not exempt the rulers of the land, which Jeremiah must be bold to deliver.

What is our natural reaction when calamities fall on us (13:22 cf 16:10)? We ask, "Why have these things come upon me?" as if we were innocent. **Where does the blame lie (13:22-27, 14:10, 16:11-13)?** The greatness of their iniquity is to blame. It is describing a spiritual disease that makes us unable to repent due to long-term indulgence of our lusts and vices. The root is in their forgetting God and trusting in lies (v25). Do not blame God; wilful sinners who will not repent are their own murderers.

God's judgement is set in motion and is not reverted. Jeremiah's ministry is about ministering to a people facing judgement: understanding their situation, how to get through the hard times, and future hope that lies ahead in restoration.

Questions for reflection:

What does prayerlessness reflect? How do you combat it?

What is your current season of life? How is it working out your faith?

From where did God pluck you up and bring you home to Him?

SESSION FIVE

Jeremiah 14-20

I. Feeling the heat, both physically and emotionally (Chs. 14-16)

A severe drought was upon the land: there was no water, no rain and no vegetation. Both man and animals suffered the same plight. They mourned and lamented (14:2). **Does it suggest that the people finally grasped God's message?** No, the people failed to realise that it was a foretaste of the coming judgement. They mourned for their trouble and not for their sin.

What did Jeremiah do for the people (14: 7-9)? He prayed for the people, which was against God's instruction. **What sentiment does it show?** It is very hard to see your kinsmen suffer. **What did Jeremiah appeal to in his prayers (14:7-9, 19-22)?** He admitted on behalf of the nation that they had sinned. He appealed to God's honour and faithfulness. For His name's sake, don't make His people a horror among the nations but remember the covenant. **How did God reply (14:10-11, 17-18)?** God reiterated His instruction to Jeremiah not to pray for the welfare of this people. Without repentance, their relationship remains broken and He won't accept any plea. He was not going to relent on His judgement which had been set to be terror.

What specific plea did Jeremiah put forward to God and did it stand (14:13-16)? In defence of the people, Jeremiah pleaded that the people had been deceived by the false prophets who had reassured them of peace. But God rebutted it in v14: ample of warnings against them had been issued but ignored. The people walked in the deceit of their hearts, which would be their ruin. **Application: can we make the same plea before God of being deceived or ignorant today?** It is a stark warning to us because we have so much more light than the people then. It is not just that we are after the first advent of Christ but also that we have so many resources accessible to us, not to say that the Bible is the best-seller of all times!

On whose sin was this severe sentence grounded (15:4)? For the sins of Manasseh, king of Judah, was Jerusalem destroyed. It means that God had withheld His judgement in leniency already but the people did not use the period of grace to repent. God would not relent now, even if Moses and Samuel, two of God's great favourite intercessors, stood before Him. **What was their punishment (16:13)?** God gave them up to their own way (serving other gods); their sins became their punishment.

God depicted three ways to die (pestilence, sword and famine) and one way to live (captivity) (15:2). All creatures are instruments of God's judgement (Calvin, *Institutes*, 3:25:12). *Pestilence, sword and famine* are a combination repeated in the Bible to emphatically convey that there is no escape from His judgement; those who are to perish will perish. Famine is probably the most torturous way to die in the situation (see also 19:9; Lam 4:9), while captivity torturous way to live in prolonged misery and humiliation. Both great and small shall die in this land (16:6) and God will silence the place (16:9) – no voice of mirth or mourning.

In view of such horror, what is Jeremiah's struggle (15:10-21 cf Ps 120:7)? Jeremiah confessed frailty of his flesh, which shows that the task of a minister is burdensome on human strength and cannot be fulfilled except by the power of God through His Spirit. Judgement is one extremely unpopular message. As the details unfolded, the severity shocked Jeremiah and upset him exceedingly that he himself seemed to have difficulty in processing it. He envisaged strife and contention that the message would stir when all he longed for was to live peaceably. He feared for his life and was sentenced to loneliness (v17). *I am for peace, but when I speak, they are for war!* (Ps 120:7) People treated the prophets harshly to silence them, believing that if they stopped prophesying, the truth would go away. The men of his hometown thought precisely like that and plotted against Jeremiah (11: 18-21). **How did Jeremiah find silence?** *Tasting* is not *eating*. Jeremiah *eats* God's words and find them nourishing, a joy and delight of his heart (v16). Silence therefore causes the prophet unceasing pain and incurable wounds (v18). **How was he cured (v19)?** God restored him if he uttered what was precious, though most unpopular, and not what was worthless, void of God's truth. God promises deliverance: "There are many things that appear very frightful that yet do not prove at all hurtful to a good man." (Matthew Henry commentary) **Application: bible study is *tasting*. Do we *eat* or chew on the words like Jeremiah and find them joy and delight to our hearts? Are we mute?**

How did God order Jeremiah to live (16:2)? To live as he preached. Here Jeremiah was ordered to stay single as a sign of the coming judgement to reinforce the message to the people by his lifestyle.

Immediately after the horror scenes of judgement is the promise of deliverance. Why is deliverance from Babylon a greater act than deliverance from Egypt (16:14-15 cf Rev 18)? Captivity in Babylon is harsher than slavery in Egypt as it is a punishment, and God's pardoning mercy is most glorious. Compared with the physical signs and wonders in Exodus, the return of the exiled Jews to Jerusalem seemed like a non-event and it is hard to imagine that it eclipses Exodus. But if deliverance from Babylon points us to Rev 18, then we understand that Exodus is a shadow of the Great Deliverance accomplished by the gospel of Jesus Christ. When the reality is here, of course the shadow is not remembered. That is why deliverance from Babylon will eclipse exodus from Egypt.

The text continues to show in 16:16-21 God's power and authority in His judgement.

II. Conviction of sin (Chs. 17-20)

Why are we always shocked when we find ourselves in judgement (17:9-10 cf 16:17-18)? Our heart is so deceitful and desperately sick that we can't know it ourselves. We always think that we are better than we really are. We are always partial to ourselves in judgement. It is always someone else's fault and not our own. We are therefore confounded how someone could find so much wrong in us. Conviction of sin needs to be well-timed, well-guided and well-managed by the Spirit, who searches our hearts, knows all our ways (v10) and brings us into Christ. Nothing is concealed from Him, so His judgement is just. **What are the effects of the conviction of sin (17:12-18)?** We run to our sanctuary and refuge knowing the disaster ahead. We plead for healing, not a patch-up job but real healing only God can do. **What does God use to show the impiety of people (17:19-27)?** The Jews in the time of Jeremiah did not even bother to pretend to be religious with external worship as before but openly violated the Sabbath. They did not hide their mischief

41

either but paraded in the public place like by the gates of Jerusalem. It was an open insult to God that (1) they despised the law, and (2) they scorned His favour and blessing as Sabbath is a gift of rest. It signifies they would consecrate nothing for God.

What do the potter and the clay depict about God's relationship with His people (18:1-4)? God is sovereign over His people, whose identity is found solely in His purpose for them. He can do as He pleases. It is God's will that prevails. As He can lift them up as a great nation among others, equally He can make their land a horror, a thing to be hissed at forever (18:16, 19:8) as an indictment of the stubbornness of their evil heart (18:12).

How do you explain the turn in Jeremiah's attitude towards the people (18:19-23)? Jeremiah knew how he had served his people and yet all his labour had been futile. It did nothing but to prove God's point about them that they were ripe for destruction. Their contempt of the prophecies only added to their sins. Their conduct had brought Jeremiah in line with God.

Jeremiah was sent to repeat the message in Valley of the Son of Hinnom. What is the significance of the place? It was the place of the vilest practice which combined idolatry with murder. It was a place filled with innocent blood, which God will avenge. *He will bring back on them their iniquity and wipe them out for their wickedness* (Ps 94:23), *woe to the wicked! It shall be ill with him, for what his hands have dealt out shall be done to him* (Is 3:11). God often makes men's sins their punishment (16:11-13). V10-11 the breaking of flask marks no return.

Who perpetrated Jeremiah's first physical affliction (20: 1)? Was what was done to Jeremiah just? Of all people, it was Pashhur, the priest, who should be in support of Jeremiah's ministry, not against it. What was done to Jeremiah was totally unjust. It followed none of the formal procedure of justice. Jeremiah was subject to beating and the public humiliation of being put in stocks in display. But his message of judgement remained unchanged (20:3-6). **How do you compare Jeremiah's lamentations in 15:10ff and 20:7ff?** Ch. 15 seemed to be Jeremiah's contemplation, which had served well as a rehearsal for the open opposition in Ch. 20 and he was more ready for it. He overcame his timidity, feeling the fire burning in his heart (20:9, echoing 15:18) that God's counsel must burst forward and could not be shut in even in face of persecution. There was an elation to find courage when needed and proved that God and all He had promised was true. He could praise Him amid affliction. God had delivered him not just from physical affliction but also from the inward distress of his mind which he recalled in v14-18.

Applications:

Tasting is not chewing; what is your experience of chewing God's Word? *In every way you were enriched in him in all speech and all knowledge* (1 Cor 1:5). How has it transformed your speech and knowledge?

Look at 17:5-8. Are you a blessed man or a cursed man? What are your struggles? Are you well connected to your fountain of living water?

What is your deepest hurt awaiting healing? Would you pray 17:14?

SESSION SIX

Jeremiah 21-23

Armed for war (1:18-19) and confronting falsehood

For the weapons of our warfare are not of the flesh but have divine power to destroy strongholds. We destroy arguments and every lofty opinion raised against the knowledge of God, and also every thought captive to obey Christ, being ready to punish every disobedience, when your obedience is complete (2 Cor 10:4-5). This is a pressing matter for all generations. This session and the next we see how Jeremiah is armed for war in order to confront falsehood and opposition. In his action, we see the shadow of Christ when He walked on earth.

What is the basis of Jeremiah's confidence (20:11)? *The Lord is with me as a dread warrior; therefore my persecutors will stumble; they will not overcome me.*

Chs. 21-29 have specific time references, but the text is not placed in the chronological order. It is therefore helpful to refresh our memory on the historical background to the text and have the time line in front of us.

Towards the end of 600s BC, the Assyrian Empire which had dominated the whole of ancient Near East was crumbling. The nations and people conquered no longer accepted their subjugation to the Assyrians. Among them were the big players, Egypt and Babylon. The Babylonians, the coming power, began to attack the Assyrians and captured their capital in 614 BC. They went on to take some other cities as well. The Egyptians moved north to aid the Assyrians against the Babylonians, but they were stopped by King Josiah of Judah who died in battle at Megiddo (2 Kings 23:28-29). As a result, Pharaoh took over authority in Judah. He removed Josiah's successor Jehoahaz (reigned only for 3 months) and put Jehoiakim on the throne instead. Judah became a buffer state between Egypt and Babylon. In 605 BC (4th year of Jehoiakim's reign), Egypt and Babylon faced each other in a big battle at Carchemish (46:2), in which the Egyptians were defeated and authority over Judah was transferred to the Babylonians.

The exile of Judah took place in stages. There were three deportations in total. The first one was in 605BC (first year of Nebuchadnezzar), when Daniel and his friends were taken. The second deportation took place in 597BC (8th year of Nebuchadnezzar), when Ezekiel was taken. The final destruction of Jerusalem and the Temple took place in 586 BC under Nebuchadnezzar.

Babylon itself did not last long after that. It fell to the Medes and Persians in 539BC. Jeremiah prophesied that seventy years must pass before the end of the desolations of Jerusalem. This was fulfilled in the first year of Cyrus king of Persia (2 Chron 36:22-23) which was 538BC. From 605BC (the first year of their subjugation to the Babylonian authority) to 538BC is 67years.

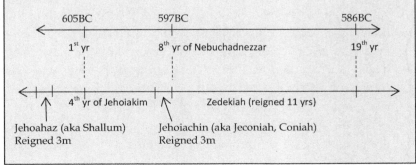

I. Message to the kings (Chs. 21-22)

In last session, we saw Jeremiah suffer physical beating and public humiliation (Ch. 20). His fate seems to have turned in Ch. 21. **What was the occasion that brought ears of the king to him (21:1-2, 2 Kings 24:20b, 25:1-2, 2 Chron 36:11-13)?** Going against Jeremiah's advice, Zedekiah rebelled against the king of Babylon. Babylon was making war against Judah. The siege would last 18 months with the final destruction of Jerusalem by fire and the end of his reign. **Can you say that his approach to Jeremiah was sincere?** 2 Chron 36 tells us that Zedekiah never listened to Jeremiah; *he stiffened his neck and hardened his heart against turning to God.* He realized he was in deep trouble with Babylon, but his reading of his plight was spiritually uninformed. In his desperation he wanted Jeremiah to use his clout as a man of God to somehow enlist God's favour to avert the attack and granted them peace. All he cared was to clear their trouble and not to reconcile with God. There was no sign of remorse or repentance of their sins. This was a self-centred way to approach God, treating God as a genie to serve him as the master. **Will God grant his request?** No, we cannot approach God in our terms but in His terms. Despite Jeremiah's persistent ministry, Zedekiah was still proud and did not register that their sins were the root cause of their calamity.

In his reply (21:3-7), what can you infer about Jeremiah's integrity as God's messenger? If he were in any way tempted by worldly ambition, this would have been the best opportunity to flatter the king and earn his high opinion. Yet he knew everything was fleeting in this world under God's judgement, so it was not temptation to him at all. Instead, his message was consistent and remained unaltered by the circumstances. His reply reflected the integrity of God's truth. His lips had been sealed by God for His prophecy and no other. He was direct and blunt, offering no compromise or softening. It had no dressing whatsoever, and employed no art of diplomacy. It was plain. Even when he uttered the last thing they wanted to hear, it was out of his love for them because understanding brought comfort in a bid to awaken them to the right course of action. His character contrasted that of the false prophets we are to encounter later in this session.

In what sense was Jeremiah's advice to the people counterintuitive (21:8-10)? We naturally think that being captured by our enemies and brought to the foreign land under their charge is the ill-fate. It rules in our favour if our home and life are intact. But Jeremiah's advice was the opposite. *The way of life* was found in the way they did not want to go. Staying where they thought safe and their protection was *the way of death*.

Jeremiah also gave a direct message to the king, which has two parts. What was the key duty of the king highlighted by Jeremiah (21:11 cf 22:3, Dan 4:27, 1 Pet 2:14)? Do justice and righteousness. The decency of a kingdom is reflected by the life of the weak and powerless, who God cares about. Law and justice are not functioning if it does not safeguard the most vulnerable. **Where did the king put his confidence (21:13-14)?** Jerusalem boasted the natural defence of Jerusalem of being in a valley and guarded with mountains, making it difficult for an army to approach (Ps 125:2). Thinking that their city was impregnable gave the king and the people a false sense of security that they scoffed, "Who shall be against us?" (v13). Our thinking should be that if God is for us, who can be against us; and if God is against us, who can be for us? Nothing is to our advantage if God is against us.

Ch. 22 appears to be an earlier sermon preached at court in some preceding reigns. **Comparing 22:3 with 21:12, what can you conclude about the character of God's judgement?** God instructs first before judgement, so that we don't have self-defence. When God judges, our mouths are stopped. **As the**

kings of Judah have failed to fulfil their stately duties towards God, what is the fate of Jerusalem (22:6-9 cf Lam 2:15)? NB: Gilead was the chief city of the ten tribes, rich and fruitful, and Lebanon was the queen of that land, especially famous for its cedars. The present prosperity and fruitfulness is no guarantee of future prosperity. The country that is now fruitful as Gilead shall be made a wilderness; the cities that are now strong as Lebanon shall be cities not inhabited. Once *the perfection of beauty and the joy of all the earth* (Lam 2:15) will lie waste and become a byword among the nations. Such contrast evokes the most heart-wrenching lamentation by Jeremiah.

In the context of 22:11-12, *weep not for* **whom and** *weep bitterly for* **whom in verse 10? Why?** Weep not for Josiah who was dead, not grieve for him, but wept bitterly for Jehoahaz (Shallum) who was taken to Egypt, never to return but died in Egypt. Josiah died reconciled with God, so he died in peace. We have confidence that he has gone home to the Lord, a far better place. In contrast, Jehoahaz had no such peace. That he died as an alien in the foreign land signifies the restlessness of the souls of those who are not reconciled with God. While dying saints can anticipate bliss this world does not know, living sinners are to be pitied. **Application: This is the toughest spiritual reality to contemplate for our unbelieving family and friends. Do you have any wisdom to share?**

22:18 implies that v13-17 is about Jehoiakim. **What kind of king was he (22:13-17 cf Lev 19:13, Deut 24:15)? What had he neglected doing?** His kingship relied on external pomp and splendour to puff up. His quest for grandeur reflected his inner insecurity. He probably pursued his grand building projects beyond his means because he did not pay his workers, suggesting injustice. This was an oppressive regime when the people served the king rather than the king in the service of the people. It was a statement that he disagreed with his father's priority which was to do justice and righteousness, to judge on the cause of the poor and needy. **What is the way to know God (22:16)?** When we seek to fulfil the duty to God in our appointed station in life, we have to understand what is expected of us and in turn to have the affection to conduct the duty in obedience as an act of worship. This is the same for all believers and not just for the kings. **What was the fate of Jehoiakim (22:18)?** He died a miserable death with no decent burial and no one to mourn for him.

The destruction of Judah was gathering pace. God is returning their way on their own head. **What was it (22:20-23 cf Ps 20:7-8, 33:16-17, 146:3-4)?** God leaves them to their strongholds that they have put their trust in: their wealth, resources, allies (lovers) and all the advantages that God had given them. They all failed Judah, which was to be pitied when she went through the pangs. **What is the curse of God's riches (22:21 cf Deut 8:17-19)?** We love the gifts and not the Giver. The riches we enjoy often make us grow proud and in contempt of God's Word. Prosperity often makes us deaf to God.

Coniah reigned for three months after Jehoiakim. His name was deliberately shortened here to show contempt. **What was the sign God gave of their broken relationship (22:24-25)?** The signet ring of a king represents his authority. Judah was chosen as God's signet ring among the nations, close and dear to God, giving Judah her honour and dignity. But they had spoilt that call and persistently refused to listen to God. So God tore it off His right hand showing that Judah was no longer worthy of that position. Their fate of destruction was sealed. It is painful for any relationship to come to this.

II.   The mischiefs of the false prophets (Ch. 23)

But false prophets also arose among the people, just as there will be false teachers among you, who will secretly bring in destructive heresies, even denying the Master who bought them, bringing upon themselves swift destruction (2 Peter 2:1)

Beloved, do not believe every spirit, but test the spirits to see whether they are from God, for many false prophets have gone out into the world... They are from the world; therefore they speak from the world, and the world listens to them (1 John 4:1, 5).

Apostle Peter makes the connection that we have much to learn about false teachers of our days from the false prophets of Jeremiah's days! Like Jesus, Jeremiah's ministry required him to confront the shepherds of Israel. Following the judgement on the kings was the judgement on the false prophets.

What does God expect the shepherds to fulfil in their ordained office (Malachi 2:5-9)? Why was God so appalled with the shepherds of Israel (23:1-2, 11, 13-14)? As shown by Jeremiah, the lips of the priests are sealed by God as His messengers in guarding knowledge. Their duty is to provide *true instruction* which springs from their fear of God and has the effect of turning many from iniquity and giving life and peace to people. The shepherds of Israel corrupted the covenant teaching and had caused many to stumble by their instruction with their partiality. The direct end result of their ministry was the scattering of the sheep entrusted to them and driving them away from their land, which God attributed to them as their evil deeds, and for that they were judged.

God's steadfast love never fails. **How does God remain faithful to His covenant (23:3-8 cf 16:14-15)? Who is this "righteous branch" (Is 11:1)?** Although the destruction seemed comprehensive, God says it was not a full end. It is always His plan that a remnant will be preserved and their restoration is promised. God will raise up faithful shepherds to take care of them, so that none of them will be missing; there will be no more fear and they will have no lack. Christ is the righteous branch because He is our righteousness. Since the kings, the prophets and the priests have all failed. Christ replaces them all in His three offices to establish justice and righteousness in the land. He is a branch which started small but rises to cover the whole world victorious. This deliverance from exile in sin and their restoration in the Promised Land, i.e. the gospel message, is infinitely greater than Israel's great exodus from Egypt that the latter ceases to be the talking point.

What is the fate of the land (23:10) and the shepherds (23:12, 15, 19-20)? The whole creation groans under judgement of our sins, and Apostle Paul tells us that it eagerly awaits with us the day of our full restoration when it is finally set free from the bondage of corruption. The shepherds will be left in darkness, and the year of their punishment is certain when disaster will strike. God's wrath depicted as a tempestuous storm has irreversibly gone forth, which cannot be stopped until it has run its course to accomplish destruction on them.

These false prophets come out of the house of God. What is the biggest lie they keep telling the people (23:16-17, 23-24)? What kind of mentality does their teaching cultivate in the wicked (Ps 36:1-3, Ps 64:5, Is 47:10)? The biggest lie that Satan tells us even to this day is that sins have no consequence, *filling them with vain hopes* to encourage sins. It will be well with us, they say, telling us that there is peace when there is no peace. The mentality of the wicked is that God does not see or know what they do. To that God answers bluntly in verses 23-24 that He is omnipresent and omniscience, He is everywhere present and all-knowing. **Are the people the innocent victims (23:26, 28 cf 2 Thess 2:10)?** The people are equally guilty because they follow *the deceit of their own heart. They refuse to love the truth and be saved.* What has straw in common with wheat? Can't they tell the difference? One is nourishing and satisfies your hunger while the other is worthless and blown away in the wind. **What is God's Word likened to (23:29)?** Fire and Hammer. To the unfaithful it is a consuming fire while to the faithful it is a refining fire. Fire hardens clay, but softens wax; it consumes the dross but purifies the gold; *to one a fragrance from death to death, to the other a fragrance from life to life* (2 Cor 2:16). If the heart cannot be melted by the word of God as the fire, it will be broken to pieces by it as the hammer. Whatever opposition is given to the word, it will be borne down and broken to pieces. **Why is their ministry so damaging and their sins so grievous (23:27-32)?** We can interpret *dream* as human fancies. It leads people to forget God (v27). They employ two devices: promote false gods and to misrepresent the true God. False prophets in God's name may do more mischief to the true religion and godliness than false prophets in Baal's name, as they confuse the true doctrines with counterfeits, hypnotizing people into a false sense of security when they actually are not saved. Paul has nothing but strongest words for false teachers – let them be accursed (Gal 1:8-9). Jesus warns us of them, calling them ravenous wolves in sheep's clothing (Matt 7:15). **Why did Jeremiah mourn for them in 23:9 (cf Ps 76:7)?** Jeremiah was more concerned about their fate than themselves because he had a better vision of their plight. Even those that have God for them cannot but tremble to think of the misery of those that face God's wrath. **Application: How do you safeguard yourself against false prophets (see e.g. John 16:13-14, Matt 7:15-16, Mark 13:22, 1 John 4:1-6)?**

Why is the phrase *the burden of the LORD* **(translated as** *the oracles of the LORD* **in NIV) cause such a great offence to God (23:33-40 cf 2 Cor 2:16 & Ps 19:10)?** This is a shameful proverb, which brands God's word with disgrace. The despisers of God perceive a prophecy as threatenings on them with vengeance, hence a burden, always bearing hard on them, teasing them and frightening them. They make the word of God a burden to themselves, and then quarrel with the ministers for making it a burden to them (like Zedekiah). The Word of God that gives life and understanding should be deemed sweet and delightful, wholesome, bearing the good news of salvation offered by His lovingkindness to us. People who chant it as a burden reflect their bitterness and hatred towards it. The fault is in our thorny heart if we see it as a burden. Their attitude reflects their heart condition, so if any of us perverts God's Word by chanting it *the burden of the LORD*, then it will really be a burden to us.

Application:

Do you approach God and demand that He gives you what you want like Zedekiah?

Do you seek God with your whole heart (24:7, 29:13)?

Is God's Word a burden or a delight to us? Is it sweeter than honey that we cannot have enough? Do you marvel what treasure God has placed into our hands?

How do you tell wheat from straw (23:28)?

SESSION SEVEN

Jeremiah 24-29

I. Humility learnt from humiliation - counsel to the people (Chs. 24-25)

Following God's message to the kings and the false prophets, we have a record of God's counsel to the people. This section expands on 21:8-10. This prophecy was given after the second deportation of Judah to Babylon which ended Jeconiah's reign. Apart from shifting the material treasures out of Jerusalem, elites and craftsmen were taken. **How did it leave Jerusalem (24:1)?** The city was almost empty, desolate compared with her former splendour. Apart from being impoverished a great deal, the depletion of their cream of human capital weakened the city further in their ability of wealth creation as well as defence.

In face of the decline in the city, God gave the sound of consolation. It was a story of two figs. **Who were the good figs and who were the bad (Ch. 24) and why (24:5)?** The people who had been sent into exile were represented by the good figs and those who remained in the city the bad figs. We know that they were all bad in and of themselves. The difference was in God's sovereign will – *I will regard as good the exiles from Judah* (v5). This was the difference. God then lists five *I will* in verses 6-7 to state what He will do for that group of people. Those are great promise of restoration, pointing to the heart-work of the new covenant in v7 that *I will give them a heart to know that I am the LORD, and they shall be my people and I will be their God, for they shall return to me with <u>the whole heart</u>*. This speaks of a new chapter in their relationship when the previous one proves disastrous in people's hands. He will work the calamity for their good. In contrast, those who stayed behind would face the terrible judgement in full to wipe them out.

How is this teaching counterintuitive? If you were the original audience, which one would you think a better fortune: exile or stay put? The people who got to remain in Jerusalem believed that they were the better people who had been spared of God's vengeance. They believed that the captivity was the punishment and they gloated on their superiority even though they were reduced to great poverty also. They had been spared for a time but they had not used it wisely for repentance. They clang onto their past glory which had enslaved them and they continued to live in their pride which had proven to be deadly for their spiritual health. In the end they faced the full vengeance of punishment until they are *utterly destroyed from the land* (v10). Those who had been sent into exile learnt humility and submission through their humiliation. **How does God work it out for their good (Job 36:15, Ps 119:67&71)?** Punishment is retrospective on making retribution for our wrongdoings, while discipline is forward looking driven by the purpose and intention in our development. Calvin distinguishes punishment from chastisement. The latter proceeds more from love than anger although we may not see it that way. Adversity breaks our pride, a massive boulder blocking our highway to God. Jonathan Atkins, the Cabinet Minister who fell from grace, makes this comment: *Grace, like water, always flows downward, to the lowest place, what a spectacular fall from grace actually became a fall into grace* (*City Lives,* Marcus Nodder, p. 132). Striking is before healing, destruction before reconstruction.

The time marker of Ch. 25 is the fourth year of Jehoiakim, the first year of Nebuchadnezzar, which means it was 605 BC the first deportation (v1). At the time of this prophecy, Jeremiah had prophesied persistently to the people for 23 years, calling them to repentance (v3). The year 605BC marked the start of birth pains, so his prophecy about judgement on Judah was being fulfilled as they had not turned back to God. They had not listened to God's messenger of mercy, so God sent them His messenger of wrath, whom they could not despise, mock or persecute.

What was Jeremiah prophesying now (25:8-14)? Three things: what to expect about Judah and their life (all normal life will cease), how long they will be in exile (70 years) and the judgement on Babylon (which fell in 539BC). **What is the significance of "seventy years" (2 Chron 36:21, Lev 26: 40-45)?** God does not only have purpose for His people in exile but also for the land which shall enjoy its Sabbath rest. Therefore Jeremiah's prophecy was nothing new but followed God's law! God's Word is truly valuable and such a marvellous guide to us!

Did other nations escape judgement (25:14-38)? The agents of God's judgement are themselves subject to judgement (v14). The agent of punishment Babylon was in turn punished for their own sins against Judah. The cup of wrath will be poured out on Judah's enemies, who will face similar devastation as Judah has. **Why is the cup of wrath likened to the cup of wine (25:16)?** We will lose the use of our reason and our minds confused. There will be alarms of all sorts: fall and rise of fortunes, wars, natural disasters, scarcity and devastation. We become paranoid and agitated. We stagger in our steps and we tremble at the outlook. We are sick. **How is the prophecy received (25:28)?** They will refuse the cup of wrath as if they could stop it from being poured out on them. They dismiss it as if it were not there. Even if they believe there is such a thing, they don't believe it will fall on them: How dare God to judge me! They sneer. Of course, what God has said, He will do and they can't refuse it.

II. Encounter oppositions (Chs. 26-28)

The time marker of Ch. 26 is back to the beginning of Jehoiakim's reign, which was 609BC, before the first deportation. Jeremiah was sent to prophesy in the court of the Lord's house which was visited by all the cities of Judah who came to worship.

What did God command Jeremiah not to do (26:2)? *Do not hold back a word!* Jeremiah was sent to the people "urgently" (v5) or "again and again" in NIV. **Application: How is this a challenge to our mindset?** Truth without love is hypocrisy; love without truth is sentimentality. Speaking the truth in love is not easy. It takes spiritual maturity. How often do we hold back God's message to people in fear of it being offensive? Do we tone down our message? The liberal Christians do that on industrial scale.

What was the reaction he received (26:7-9)? Hostility from the religious leaders. They sentenced him to death on the charge of blaspheming the city, the Holy Place. **How did Jeremiah defend against the distorted charge (26:12-15)?** They deliberately left out the part that their sins played in condemning the city to ruin. They clang on to their sins and wanted to silence the critic. **When Jeremiah stood against the charges, how did he show he was a worthy servant of God? How did he compare with Uriah (26:20-23)?** Jeremiah did not compromise the message given to him. He was fearless, trusting in God, either to deliver him or He would avenge his blood (v15). He was at peace with that. In contrast Uriah prophesied a similar message to Jehoiakim but he did not trust in God's protection. He tried to protect himself by plotting an escape to Egypt which offered him no protection at all and he met a dishonoured death in the hands of the king. **How did the officials argue that Jeremiah did not deserve to die (26:16-23)?** Micah prophesied during the reign of Hezekiah who did not kill him but repented and averted the disaster. **In the end, who was the person God arranged to deliver Jeremiah (26:24 cf 2 Kings 22:12)?** Ahikam the son of Shaphan. He was a minister in Josiah's government and his father was the secretary. We have confidence then Ahikam was a godly man like the king he served was. Remember this name as we will meet his family further on. God providence works for His saints. **Application: whom are we reminded of in this encounter?** A type of Christ.

The time marker for Chs. 27 and 28 is the start of Zedekiah's reign in 597BC. It means that the second deportation has just taken place, including much of the vessels of the temple. **What was Zedekiah plotting (27:3)?** He was plotting rebellion against Babylon by calling a summit of neighbouring nations who sent their envoys to Jerusalem. **What was Jeremiah's message to all the kings (27:2-11)?** At the outset of this message God stated His right of making the command (v5), proclaiming His sovereign right over all things. God commanded Jeremiah to make and wear straps and yoke-bars to bring home God's message to all nations that they submitted to the yoke of Babylon and served their king. If they did, they would remain in their land and do well. If they didn't, they would be banished from their land and perish. **What was his message to Zedekiah (27:12-15)?** Same as other nations of submission to the yoke of Babylon. In addition, do not listen to the false prophets (v14) and Jeremiah told him how to discern them by their messages. The stripping of the Temple, which was the Jews' pride and confidence, was a strong sign that God had departed. The false prophets wanted to pacify them that it would be a short exile and the treasures of the Temple would be returned in two years, compared with three generations (v7). This was what the people wished to believe.

One such false prophet was Hananiah who foretold that the yoke would be broken within two years. **How did Jeremiah confront him (28: 5-9 cf Deut 18:21-22)?** He would be exposed when what he prophesied did not come to pass. Hananiah took his wooden yoke and smashed it to reiterate his prophecy. God punished the false teachers.

III. Letter to the exiles (ch 29)

Ch. 29 is parallel to Chs. 24 and 25 in content. The latter was prophesied to the people remaining in Jerusalem while this chapter was the same message of the two figs in a letter sent to the people in exile to encourage them. The letter was delivered by Zedekiah's officials. One of them was Elasah, son of Shaphan, therefore brother to Ahikam who saved Jeremiah from his death sentence (26:24). Apostle Peter identifies us as sojourners and exiles in this world (1 Peter 2:11). God's counsel to Judah in exile has relevance to us in this context.

Why did Jeremiah feel the need to write to the exiles (29:8)? There were false prophets among them. Hearing God's truth is life and death. **What was his advice to the exiles (29:4-7, 28)? What would have otherwise been their attitude?** They were asked to settle down and lead a normal life. "Do not be impatient to go and overlook the opportunity to do good to the neighbour and in the community." They were asked to seek the welfare of the city, as their welfare was tied to it. In other words, do not live to sabotage the authority and see them as enemies. This was madness to some people (29:26). **How did God work their adversity to make them become the good figs (29:10-14)?** Trust in His plan which works only to prosper them and not to harm them. They have a future and hope in His promise. He will bring them back; He will gather them from all nations and restore their fortunes. In their vulnerability, they will learn about their total dependence on God who will not fail them. Communion with God will be established with the people calling upon God, drawn to Him and pray to Him, and God will hear. God promises to be found when they seek Him (v13-14). **Why did God tell them about those remaining in Jerusalem (29:15-23)?** God also tells them life that they fantasize is not real. The pasture is not greener over the other side. In fact it could be worse. **How were their brothers back home bad figs?** They paid no attention to God's words, continued to oppose His messengers sent to them for their good, remained adulterous and kept lying in God's name, thinking that God did not know their acts. But God confirms that He is the witness and He is the one who knows. The exiles were the "lucky" ones to escape the terror of judgement in sword, famine and pestilence. **Was there opposition to Jeremiah's message to the exiles (29:24-32)?** God's way is not our way and His thought is not our thought. For those whose hearts are hardened, God's message does not make sense. Jeremiah duly pronounced Shemaiah the fate of false prophets.

Questions for reflection:

What is the greatest comfort you learn from God in this session?

Do you believe that God works all things for your good (Rom 8:28) or do you struggle to believe it?

When you find yourself in an unexpected place in life, do you respond as good figs?

SESSION EIGHT

Jeremiah 30-33

Sound of comforts

After much sound of thunders, we have come to the section which is the balm for the afflicted people's souls if they care to listen. It stretches our horizon and lifts it beyond here and now. God reveals His purpose to us, which gives meaning to everything.

I. The promise of restoration (Ch. 30)

Why did God ask Jeremiah to write down His words in a book (30:2)? (1) In a scroll rather than in a letter is for keeping and passing down, lest people forget and have no hope. (2) Enable people to check its fulfilment to strengthen people's faith and know their God. The original audience did not believe Jeremiah, or they were still expecting their return would happen within two years. Daniel's prayer in Dan Ch. 9 was based on Jeremiah's prophecy of 70 years. (3) It has relevance well beyond the immediate generations. It points to Christ. **What is the difference between (30:3) and (28:3)?** Both false and true prophets prophesy a restoration of fortune but the timing is God's (also in v8) and not our human wishful thinking, 70 years versus two years.

Note that the prophecy concerns both Israel and Judah (30:4). How did the prophecy begin (30:4-7)? People are reminded of the terror of judgement, whereby God strikes and reduces all men to a condition not manly, such as a woman in labour (v6). When there are fights without, there are fears within. Seeing the strong defence of the nation collapse in haste, even the strongest men used to actions and fixing things are reeling under helplessness. All the self-reliance is gone; all pride is crushed. Make no mistake, the destruction of Jerusalem is a horror. **Why is the pain and groan likened to that of a woman in labour and not of a deathbed?** Unlike a deathbed, after pains and groans in labour is life. The time of Jacob's distress is terrible, *yet he shall be saved out of it* (v7). Though the affliction of the church may last long, they shall not last always.

What are people saved to do (30:9 cf Ex 8:21)? So who will be saved? "Let my people go, that they may serve me (Ex 8:21)". We are not saved such that we can live our own life but that we give up our life to serve our Lord. So the hope and comfort is for the faithful. **Whom are the people to serve?** David the king had been dead for a long time. There were not any successors on the throne after the destruction of Jerusalem. The Jews had long been so taught that they were to place their whole confidence as to their salvation on David, i.e. on the king whom God had set over them. It was not that David was able by his own power to save the people, but because he typically personated Christ. This points to Christ. The Lord their God is also their King David.

Restoration: the nation: **What can you deduce as the people's fears from 30:10-11?** They are all scattered and they fear that

God may not be able to gather them all up. God reassures them that He knows His own and He will not miss any one of them. The harshness of punishment feels like the end. But God says that the punishment on Jacob's enemies will mark a full end of them but not for Jacob. **What is the difference between punishment received by *you* (Jacob) and *all the nations* in 30:11?** Calvin (in *Institutes*, 3:4:31) makes a distinction between judicial punishment and judicial chastisement. Divine punishment is accompanied with indignation. Divine vengeance is poured on God's enemies, confounding, scattering, and annihilating them. In judicial chastisement, God is offended but not in wrath; he does not punish by destroying or striking down as with a thunderbolt. Hence it is not purely punishment, but also correction and admonition. The former is the act of a judge, the latter of a father. When Jeremiah pleads, "Correct me, O LORD, but in justice; not in your anger, lest you bring me to nothing (10:24)", he is pleading for chastisement and not punishment from God. One brings them to a full end while the other not. **Whom must be destroyed completely in their ultimate deliverance?** All the enemies against His Church must meet their full end.

Restoration: wellness: Why is the infliction on Jacob so severe that *Your hurt is incurable and your wound is grievous* (30:12-15)? It is but proportionate to their sins and guilt: *Because your guilt is great, because your sins are flagrant, I have done these things to you*. **Despite their desperate condition, what is God's promise (30:17 cf Eze 37:1-14)?** The condition of the Jews in captivity was like a valley full of dead and dry bones, which nothing less than the Omnipotent can put life into. God promises them restoration to health and healing of wounds. **What is the warning to the enemies of the Church (30:16-17, 20b)?** God will avenge His people. Their contempt and scoff against His Church will fly back on their face as God will restore His Church, who will triumph over them.

Restoration: the city and life: **What can they look forward to in their city (30:18-21)?** A heap of rubble is rebuilt into a city of dwellings and palace. Sounds of merriment, gratitude and celebration fill the streets again. Enemies are purged out of the land. People multiply. They have a ruler to rule over them. **What are the characteristics of this ruler (30:21)?** The king is the soul of the people. He is one of them; He comes from their midst. God makes Him draw near and allows Him to approach Him. **Whom does this point to (cf Lev 10:3, 21:17; Ex 20:21)?** These descriptions were used for Moses as a Mediator and Aaron as the priest. This points to the priestly order of Melchizedek, i.e. a priest is also a king at the same time. **How is 30:22 fulfilled?** Therefore this refers to the spiritual offspring of Abraham subject to the kingship and priesthood of Christ in His kingdom. Through His office, Christ draws near a people to God and approach God so that v22 is fulfilled: *you shall be my people, and I will be your God*. We have discussed that this has always been God's covenant relationship with His people. This people (i.e. His church) will be the New Jerusalem, the Heavenly Jerusalem.

What is in common in all these aspects of restoration (33:14-18, Is 11:1)? There is a sense that something dead and hopeless comes back to life. Christ Himself rose up as a shoot of a tree that had been cut down as Judah had been: *There shall come forth a shoot from the stump of Jesse, and branch from his roots shall bear fruit*. Unless we direct all our thoughts to Christ, all the promises will vanish away.

After such joyous picture of restoration, are vv 23-24 out of place (cf Ps 48:11, 2 Thess 2:6-8)? The picture of the Heavenly Jerusalem is not complete if judgement on the wicked is absent. It is heaven because sin is purged and its entry barred. Similarly our joy for heaven is not complete if we do not rejoice because of God's judgements. This is not out of hatred towards the wicked but a love of God's justice and holiness, seeing it glorious. The gospel is bittersweet in the sense that we share Jeremiah's sorrow in seeing anyone face judgement. What does it take? I am afraid that it will take us tasting and witnessing as full an extent of wickedness as we can bear. God has been protecting His people by restraining the evil. What will happen in the last day? 2 Thess 2:6-8 tells us that God will get this restraining force out of the way so that the lawless one will be revealed. *In the latter days,* for both the faithful and the wicked, *will understand this* (v24).

II.   Return from captivity (31:1-20)

God gives His declaration of love in 31:3: *I have loved you with an everlasting love; therefore I have continued my faithfulness to you.* Even when God seems to have abandoned His people, He has not. **Why is it shocking that God calls Israel "virgin" in v4 & 21 and what does it mean (cf 2 Cor 11:2 & Rev 14:4)?** God has been repeatedly calling Israel a whore in Jeremiah. She has committed covenantal infidelity and shameless in her promiscuous and impudent spiritual adultery which provokes God to anger. This image is the furthest from that of a virgin. Yet in her restoration, God washes her clean and pure in the blood of Christ, and betroths her to one husband, Christ, free from defilement. We shall see how God ensures that. She will be richly adorned as the virgin bride of Christ. **People are back to merriment. What do the watchmen do (v6)?** They are not threatened with dangers. Even watchmen are reassured that they don't need to keep watch but go to worship. **God is not saving everyone but a remnant of Israel (31:7). What kind of people are they (31:7-9, 18-19)? What does God guarantee (31:9, 20)?** No matter where we are, God will find us and gather us up. His people is not one fit or perfect but lame and blind and heavily laden (v8). The remnant has responded to the correction of the captivity, knowing that they can offer nothing to stand before God except God's mercy (v9). Finally, God's chastisement has brought to them their senses and they feel guilty and ashamed, even indignant of their past sins. They respond with remorse and are confounded by their folly (v19). They come with weeping, pleading for mercy, which is in sharp contrast with how they were before – proud and stiff necked. Those are tears of repentance but also of gladness to receive mercy. <u>Do we see our image in there? We are not chosen because of our merits. We are broken and contrite, knowing that we only have God's mercy.</u> God's arm is not too short to save. He guarantees that a path will be carved out for us to get to Him and we shall not stumble (v9). The way of His people to Him is sure. **How does that conversion come about (31:18b)?** We plead with God that we may be restored. We are powerless in turning back to God ourselves. It is by God's converting grace, which opens our eyes to understanding. When sinners come to a right knowledge they will come to a right way. *For you are my God* shows it is God's peculiar favour for His elect.

While the people easily believe that they are in perpetual exile, God asks them to remember their way home (v21). What is their prospect (v22)? God asks them not to waver between gods but trust in His promise. Although to take place in the future to them, God uses past tense to signify the certainty of *a new thing he has created on earth* (as opposed to *will create* in NIV). It is our gospel hope in Christ Jesus. While the Jews were like a weak woman against the strong and mighty men of Babylon, God points them to the future that their enemies will be judged for their deeds. It foreshadows that the Church has the ultimate triumph over her strong and mighty enemies; she will besiege them. Who will perpetuate are God's people and not her enemies. **Read 31:23-30 (cf 31:10-14), what prospect did God show Jeremiah that he found it so "pleasant" (v25)?** It is a picture of spiritual blessings, peace and of no lacks. The weary souls of calamities find rest and hope. Fullness replenishes emptiness. Their life shall be like a watered garden as opposed to a broken cistern which can hold no water. Once again, joy fills up their hearts that burst out praising God in songs and dance. Rather than being the byword of the nations, they will radiate God's glory and favour on them once again. The people look forward to satisfaction after a period of sorrow and upheaval. When we see the plucking up and breaking down, God reminds Jeremiah of His promise to build and plant. *In those days* (v29) refers to the days after God had punished them. They would finally come to see God's justice as blameless. His mercy would show that everyone is worthy of death.

As Judah came to represent the Southern Kingdom, **Ephraim** represents Israel, the ten tribes, the Northern Kingdom. Ephraim was not the first-born but the younger son of Joseph. Even so, Jacob put him before Manasseh (Gen 48:20). Note that Shiloh, mentioned in (7:8-15), was in the territory of Ephraim.

31:15-16: *Ramah* was where the Chaldeans gathered the captives (see 40:1). Jacob had two wives and he loved Rachel more than Leah (Gen 29:30). Rachel bore two sons, Joseph (father of Ephraim and Manasseh) and Benjamin (one of the two tribes of the Southern Kingdom with Jerusalem in its territory). Rachel died at childbirth of Benjamin. She wished to name the baby Benoni – the son of sorrow – only to be overruled by Jacob who named him Benjamin. **Rachel** represented the mother of both kingdoms. Nothing is bitterer than a mother's weeping for the loss of her children, especially when the expectation is that "they are no more". The devastation was so horrendous that they could not visualize restoration. But God replies that the weeping and tears should be refrained as it is not the full end for they shall return from the land of the enemy. As work is rewarded, the comfort and joy from deliverance shall balance out the grievousness of their suffering in captivity. Amid this tragic grief, God is working out His purposes all along to end His people's spiritual exile, and that of Gentiles too, through Jesus Christ.

III. Hope for something even better (31:31-40)

Let's take stock of where we are in the teaching of Jeremiah so far. He has established strongly that the Jews are inexcusable in their sinning and deserve nothing but God's wrath and hell. He compares their destruction with hell. Hell is justice for them – this has been the main theme. Once they understand their state before God, they are in a position to understand God's mercy which gives them what they don't deserve. The promise of restoration is therefore incredible. Against their sins, God's love to take them back is scandalous.

What does it take for God to restore His people (31:11)? God has to redeem His people. **But from whom (Is 52:3)?** God has sold them on account of their sins. Their enemies have paid nothing for them. As such, they have no right to detain them, and can't be hindrance to their deliverance. God redeems them from His own wrath. This is what Jesus does. The debt He pays on our behalf is to God. Our enemies might look strong but do not despair.

What is even more marvellous from their viewpoint is that God not only restores them to where they were before but better it. In their despair, they would have found it hard to believe. To substantiate the truthfulness of this promise, Jeremiah tells the people that this restoration is through a new covenant.

Which is the old covenant (v32)? The one that God established with the people after the Exodus, i.e. the covenant of the Law with Moses being the Mediator. **In what sense is the New Covenant "new"?** The new covenant is not so called to suggest that it contradicts the old as God cannot be inconsistent with Himself. There is strong continuity between them, as they share the same essence. God never wavers from the purpose of the covenant that He is making a people of His own possession – they shall be my people and I shall be their God. His covenant with Abraham is confirmed by the Law and is accomplished by the New Covenant. It will be consummated in the New Jerusalem. Both the Old and the New raise the hope of the faithful to beyond the present life and hold out the sure hope of eternity. The OT looked forward to Christ while the New looks backward to the Christ as the Mediator; Christ was the pledge in the OT. The Old Covenant foreshadowed the spiritual promises of the New by earthly objects and temporal blessings to train the people and confirm them in the heavenly hope. As Hebrews explains, when the reality is here, the shadow becomes obsolete. The New is in the Old concealed while the Old is in the New revealed (Augustine). We can't understand the New without the Old because of this continuity. This is why we do well in paying attention to the prophecy (2 Pet 1:19-21).

What are the differences between the Old and the New (v33-34 cf 2 Cor 3:4-6)? The Law does not save but condemn! Judah has shown us our best effort in obeying the Law – we sin most grievously – because we only follow the letter and not the spirit. The letter kills but the Spirit gives life (2 Cor 3:6). Moses' is the ministry of condemnation while the new is the ministry of righteousness (2 Cor 3:9). The Gospel brings with it the grace of regeneration that the letter from Christ in us is not written with ink but the Spirit of the living God, not on tablets of stone but on tablets of human hearts (2 Cor 3:3). With the transformation of the heart, obedience is rendered to the righteousness of God. The second difference listed here is that the outpouring of the Holy Spirit after the ascension of Christ has promised us much greater illumination than our OT counterparts. Now sin will not stand in our way as through Christ, our sins have been dealt with and God reconciled with us. We have direct access to God in Christ rather than going through the priests as in the OT. We can read and learn His Word directly rather than waiting to be instructed by the priests. (This is what you are doing right now with the study!)

While the world stands, God will have a church in it (v35-37). The earthly Jerusalem will be rebuilt when the exiles return. The boundaries of the land are marked out as sacred (vv38-40). But the New Jerusalem has no temple because it is all temple.

IV. Live out the hope you have (Ch. 32)

The time maker of the chapter is 10th year of Zedekiah's reign or 18th year of Nebuchadnezzar's reign. That is, Jerusalem had been under siege for a year. Within a year, it would be destroyed and people sent on exile in Babylon. **Why did Zedekiah lock up Jeremiah in the court of guard (32:1-5)?** He did not like what Jeremiah was prophesying about the fate of the kingdom. Still they did not believe him; still he believed that they could go against God's will. He wanted to silence him by shutting him up. He might also worry about the impact of the prophecy on the army's morale if Zedekiah wanted them to keep fighting.

At such a time as this, God instructed Jeremiah to buy a field at his hometown to keep it in the family. Jeremiah obeyed without understanding. **Why did Jeremiah find the deal perplexing (32:24-25)?** There is a lot to learn about Jeremiah's prayer but we have not got the time. It is also a very good summary of Jeremiah's ministry so far. What God had made him prophesied had come to pass. The sword, the famine and the pestilence had descended upon them in the city. Could God be relenting and spare Jerusalem if God was asking him to buy a field? Even Jeremiah, who had been prophesying restoration, had difficulty in grasping the full extent of that future vision. **What was God's reply (32:26-44)?** Jeremiah was mistaken if he thought that God was going to relent. No, the fierce anger of God was not to turn back until His intent was accomplished. His mercy is equally sure. Yet assurances of future mercy must not be interpreted as securities from present troubles. God's horizon is further than ours. **How does God bring about the restoration and why is it sure (32:37-42)?** The restoration depends on God alone and nothing on us! Of course then He can be sure because He is God the Almighty. He is committed to do good to us (v40). Even our not turning away from Him is His doing: *I will put the fear of me in their hearts, that they may not turn from me* (v40).

At the beginning of Ch. 33, the word of the LORD came to Jeremiah the second time. The time marker says that Jeremiah was still shut up in the court of guard, meaning that this was still within that last year of Judah. We see that the word of the LORD was similar to what had been said. It suggests that seeing the city which used to represent perfection and the glory of God flattened and filled up with dead bodies was really hard on His faithful. God in His compassion came and reassured Jeremiah with encouragement. **In our time of trouble and despair, where does God teach us to look (33:6-9)?** We look up to Him and all His promises. It is because we trust in Him that we trust in His promises which are characterised by "I will". God focused Jeremiah on the restoration of the city and the life within. Against brokenness, He promises healing, cleansing, forgiveness, and restoration so that the city once desolate will again fill with joy and praise.

God stretches Jeremiah vision even further. Where does God lift Jeremiah's eyes to see (33:14-26)? Beyond this life to the promise of the Messiah – the righteous branch from the stump of Jesse. Even the human world looks chaotic right now, the natural order is never upset. The reliable order of the natural world God uses to underscore His faithfulness and His unwavering commitment to all the "I will"s. **"The LORD is our righteousness" appears in 23:6 and 33:16. Who has this name respectively?** In the former reference, it is the name of the King. In here, it is the name given to the redeemed city of Jerusalem. Christ's righteousness is imputed to His people (2 Cor 5:21). We are justified in Christ's righteousness, an alien righteousness.

Applications:

Are you a *secular* Christian, focusing only on here and now? (*Seculum*, the Latin word from which we get "secular" means this age and this life. A secular Christian is one who has his hopes and concerns, even his own spiritual life, all contained in this *speculum*.)

Do you live out your eternal hope in your daily life?

Have you witnessed / experienced the restorative and healing power of Christ, the righteous Branch that springs up for David?

SESSION NINE

Jeremiah 34-39

The Fall of Jerusalem

I.   God's faithfulness and Judah's treachery (Chs. 34-35)

The chapter begins with Babylon's invasion of Judah in full force and advanced well. They were *fighting against Jerusalem and against all the cities of Judah that were left, Lachish and Azekah, for these were the only fortified cities of Judah that remained* (34:7). Zedekiah for sure had been feeling the heat of the battles. At this time, God sent Jeremiah to Zedekiah. **What was God's message to him (34:1-5)?** He reiterated the fate of Jerusalem that it would be burnt down by fire. As to the fate of the king, ill-fate was mixed with mercy: he shall die a captive, but he shall not die by the sword but a natural death (v4). He shall end his days with some comfort that he shall die in peace and he will be honoured with a burial as the former kings and people will mourn for his death (v5). **What does "dying in peace" suggest to you?** Only those who truly reconciled with God can be said to die in peace.

Does it suggest Zedekiah finally learnt the lesson of repentance like others in exile in his last days? We can't be sure. But as we shall see, he played a key role in preserving Jeremiah when his court meant him harm. Maybe there was some reverence towards God in his heart.

Zedekiah sought to address an age-old transgression that the Jews had been committing. What was the transgression, what did Zedekiah do and what was the outcome (34:8-16 cf Ex 21:2)? According to the Mosaic Law, the Jews could not enslave his own people for more than seven years. People might be held in servitude to pay off their debts or as punishment for their crimes. But they must be set free after seven years at the longest. This was a difference put between God's people and strangers. Here we see Hebrew slaves being emphasised (v9). But their fathers had been transgressing this law (v14). Staring at the fall of Jerusalem, King Zedekiah attempted to right this wrong, so he made a covenant with all the people in Jerusalem, including the officials, to set these slaves free. God accepted this as "they recently repented" and that "they did what was right in His eyes" (v15). In other words, God commended the turn. But the people changed their mind. They reversed the whole initiative and brought the male and female slaves who had been set free back into subjection as slaves.

What might have changed their mind (34:21 cf 37:5)? In dealing with His people, God never fails to demonstrate that He is slow to anger and swift to mercy. Upon the act of repentance by His people, the Chaldeans retreated from Jerusalem in face of Pharaoh's army. But when the danger of judgement appeared to be past, they fell back into their old ways. **What does it suggest about their "repentance" (Matt 24:13)?** It is not genuine from the heart. They were willing to let them go because they thought they were going to lose everything to the Chaldeans anyway. Why not cash in some free brownie points with God from a bad situation? But as soon as there was a slight possibility that this fate might have been averted, they grabbed them back. Their act of remorse was cheap. The righteousness that does not endure but is turned back on is no righteousness. Therefore, endurance of our faith proves our faith true. *But the one who endures to the end will be saved* (Matt 24:13). **What do we learn about our hardness of heart?** When we face bad fortune, we curse God. When we face good fortune, we forget God. It is just untrue that people would naturally praise God when life is going well. For those who praise Him, they will praise Him in all circumstances.

How did God take this act of the people (34:16 cf Ecc 5:4-6)? God took it as profanation of His name. It showed contempt to His law as well as the covenant they had made with Him. We must take our vow with God seriously. **What is the consequence of breaking the covenant (34:18-19 cf Gen 15: 10-11, 17)?** The making of a covenant is sealed by calling down a curse on the party who breaks it. The act was in effect saying, "May we become like this animal if we fail to keep this covenant." We see that God passed between the pieces when He made the covenant with Abraham, invoking a curse upon Himself should He fail to keep His covenant. Because He can swear by no higher authority, He swore by Himself to keep the covenantal terms. Here we see the people breaking the covenantal terms, so the penalty was that their dead bodies would be left unburied as food for the birds and wild animals (v20).

As they turned round and took back the slaves into servitude, God brought back to the city the Chaldean army which had withdrawn (34:21-22). Their way would fall upon their own heads when they would live in servitude to strangers in exile (5:19). Fire is a symbol of judgement in the Bible (after Noah's flood). In chapter 35, the obedience of the Rechabites was used to contrast the Jews' disobedience and show how inexcusable the Jews' perverseness was.

Who were the Rechabites (Ch. 35)? They were descendants of the father-in-law of Moses, i.e. originally the Midianites. Moses invited them to follow them and not to return to their land and their kindred so that they could be their guides in the wilderness and serve as eyes for them. Moses promised them an inheritance (Num 10:29-32). But as it appears from many parts of Scripture, that promise was never materialized for them and they in turn had been living as sojourners among the tribes and known as the Kenites (Judges 4:11). We read about *Jonadab* in 2 Kings 10:15-17. Jehonadab (also spelt Jonadab), the son of Rechab, was a man of great name and influence during the reign of King Jehu (841-814/3 BC). The King had him as a friend though he was an alien. He was raised up to the King's chariot to be next to him, as it were, when he was on the mission to purge the northern kingdom of Israel of wicked King Ahab's descendants. On account of the continual calamities of the land of Israel, which laid waste, and its final ruin was at hand, the descendants of Rechab had moved on to Jerusalem as we find them in Jer 35.

The time marker of Ch. 35 is "in the days of Jehoiakim", which means this scene took place before Ch. 34. Jeremiah was sent to bring the Rechabites into the house of the Lord. **How were the Rechabites living among the Jews (35: 8-9) and why?** These people were not God's people. What they were adhering to was not God's law, but what their father had taught them. Their ancient ways were summed up in four things: drink no wine, cultivate no field, plant no vineyards and build no houses. They were content with living in tents even when they moved to the city of Jerusalem. They lived in this way that "they may live many days in the land that they sojourned". In the language of OT, "living many days" means life. They carried on living in this way for only one reason – their obedience to the voice of their venerable father Jonadab. **How did this way of living contrast the lifestyle in Jerusalem (cf 6:6-7; 13:12-14)?** The city was filled with drunkenness, both physical and spiritual. It was full of violence and oppression, with injustice against the poor and the needy. The sons of Josiah were after pomp, building splendour without being able to afford it. **Why do you think Jonadah leave them commands to live a simple life?** Jonadah had seen the degenerative lifestyle of Israel and its destructive power. He passed down his wisdom to his descendants to protect them. **What is the remarkable character about Rechabites keeping Jonadab's commands?** They had kept it for nearly three centuries! We can imagine how easily it could have been challenged as not keeping pace with the time. The pressure to adapt the instruction must have been enormous in order that they made progress. The temptation to enjoy more material comfort must be irresistible especially when they lived in Jerusalem overflowing with riches and luxury. Yet the words of Jonadab carried such authority that they adhered to against the strong tides. Their submission and obedience to him must be out of love and trust rather than out of fear as in response to terror and threats. If it had been the latter, it must have long lost its grip on the people since Jonadab was long dead. **What was the purpose that Jeremiah set up the scene in the house of the Lord into the chamber of the man of God adjoined to the chambers of officials and princes (35:3-4, 12-17)?** The Rechabites were brought there to shame the Jews from the top level. What is commended here is not the rules by which the Rechabites lived but their obedience to their forefather. They were obedient to one who was but a man like themselves, who had but the wisdom and power of a man, and was only the father of their flesh; but the Jews were disobedient to an infinite and eternal God, who had an absolute authority over them, as the only Father of all. The Rechabites were obedient to someone long dead while God is a living God and kept sending prophets to His people to remind them of the way.

Applications: What is the nature of obedience highlighted? In our modern days, we demand God to convince us in reasoning before we will listen to Him. This is no real obedience to the authority. It is obedience to *our* reasoning. Real obedience is that we obey even when it does not make sense to us or when it is against our wish. In the NT children are commanded to obey their parents in the Lord for this is right (Eph 6:1). Teaching children obedience in the household is training them obedience to God. This is a tall order in Christian parenting especially in an age when we slam all authority. **What can we learn from God's will in the life of the Rechabites?** It has taken them nearly three centuries to find out that their moment to shine in God's plan was to teach us a lesson about obedience, to convict the Jews of their disobedience as indefensible and to justify their destruction. It is beyond many's lifetime! God's way is not our way and God's thought is not our thought! It is not that God is unreasonable but that we simply do not have His breadth and depth to comprehend everything. We are called to trust Him. **What did God promise the Rechabites (35:18-19)?** The Rechabites had been promised an inheritance by Moses which had never materialised until now. God says: *Jonadab the son of Rechad shall never lack a man to stand before me.* God in His timing will right all injustice and give us honour that is due to us, sometimes not in our lifetime. It stretches our horizon far and beyond. Remain faithful and God will not owe us our reward. **As Christians, we live as aliens in this world. Do we lead a distinctive lifestyle from the rest?**

II.   Judah rejected God's Word (Ch. 36)

The time marker is the fourth year of Jehoiakim (v1), the year of the first deportation to Babylon. Baruch became Jeremiah's scribe to write down what he said in a scroll. He was then to read it out at the house of God in the fifth year of the reign (v9). **What was the message (36:3, 7)?** Judgement is nigh, hoping that it would stir them into repentance and plead for mercy. **What were the people coming into Jerusalem to do (36:9)?** To fast. Ironically this was a gesture of piety and devotion which God would soon show was just a show.

The officials listened to Baruch and believed that the king should hear this. **How do you interpret the king's response upon hearing God's warning (36:2-26)? Compare 36:24 with 2 Kings 22:19.** He showed his despise of God's Word. He showed his resolve to persist in his sins and was not prepared to be corrected. The way how he burnt the scroll piece by piece showed his hostility towards God and His servants, the same kind of hostility that Jesus confronted from the religious leaders of His days. Indeed Jehoiakim commanded Jeremiah and Baruch to be seized (v26), surely to do them harm or God would not have to hide them. In sharp contrast to Josiah, his father, Jehoiakim showed no remorse or mournfulness whatsoever. Judgement was pronounced against him in v30-31. Whatever we do to God's Word, it will not be mutilated but stand. *The grass withers, the flowers fades, but the word of our God will stand for ever.* (Is 40: 8).

Application: Are we selective towards God's Word, believing what we like and dismissing what we don't like? If yes, it's no difference from tearing out pages from our Bibles.

III. The last days of Judah (Chs. 37-39)

Although *neither [King Zedekiah] nor his servants nor the people of the land listened to the words of the LORD that he spoke through Jeremiah the prophet* (37:2), the king often found himself seek out Jeremiah when he was troubled (e.g. Ch.21, 32:1-5). It must be distressing to preside over the doom days of a nation. **Against the false hope that the little respite gave, how did Jeremiah convey the certainty of God's way (37:9-10)?** What human eyes see is deceptive. God's way will prevail because His way does not depend on men. Therefore even if Judah should defeat the whole army of Chaldeans, they would still rise up with their injured men to burn the city down. It means that it is not the Chaldeans who did it but God. **How do you compare Jehoiakim's (Ch. 36) and Zedekiah's response to God's Word?**

Both want to hear what they wanted to hear from God. When they heard what they did not want to hear, Jehoiakim poured contempt on God as if his power were greater than God's and he could cancel His Word by burning it and going after His servants' life to silence His voice. In contrast, Zedekiah showed more reverence to God that he played a role in keeping His prophet alive. He also attached much weight to God's Word; he just wished that God would somehow change His mind by repeatedly seeking out Jeremiah to pray for him or consult him.

When the siege was temporarily lifted, Jeremiah tried to access a piece of land that belonged to him, perhaps the one he was asked to purchase in 32:1-15. But he was caught at the Benjamin Gate on the charge of desertion. He denied the charge, but was beaten and imprisoned nonetheless in the house of Jonathan the secretary. At length Zedekiah sought him out, probably because the Chaldeans had laid a fresh siege on the city. Jeremiah pleaded with him then that he would not send him back to the house of Jonathan. His wish was granted by the king (v21). It is an instance of the care God takes of his suffering servants that are faithful to Him. Recall God's promise to Jeremiah in 1:18-19. This was how Jeremiah ended up in the court of guard, where God reassured him of Israel's restoration as the siege deepened (Chs. 32-33).

It appears that Jeremiah had much liberty inside the court of guard as his words were still getting out to people. **Why were the princes angry with him (38:4)?** His message from God was adversely affecting the morale of the army. Those in power still believed that victory against the Chaldeans was for their good and their defeat their harm. Therefore Jeremiah was their enemy because of what he was prophesying. **In face of the death sentence announced by those in his court, what was Zedekiah's response (38:5)?** There is no doubt that Zedekiah knew Jeremiah was a true prophet from God. Yet he gave him up to his men who were hissing to vent their anger and frustration of the siege on Jeremiah. God's protection of His faithful does not rely on one man. **When Jeremiah was left sinking in the mud at the bottom of a cistern, whom did God send to rescue him (38:7-13)?** Ebed-melech the Ethiopian, who was a gentile but had more reverence to God than the Jews. He boldly declared to the king that what these princes did to Jeremiah was evil (v9). Sometimes black and white, good and evil is not hard to see but it takes courage to acknowledge. As if awakened, Zedekiah commanded, *"Take thirty men with you from here, and lift Jeremiah the prophet out of the cistern before he dies"* (Jer 38:10). The eunuch displayed much thought and tenderness in planning the rescue operation (v11-13).

In staring at defeat, what was Zedekiah's struggle (38:14-28)? As he saw the prophecy fulfilled in real life, it was hard to deny the prophecy was true. In the last hours, he sought out the truth which he knew no one would speak to him except Jeremiah. As the concern of Jeremiah (v15) suggests, he had been purging the court of people who spoke the truth. Jeremiah's counsel concerning the nation was one word: surrender. Zedekiah could not do it as he was worried about being a laughing stock and dealt with cruelly by his own people who had already deserted. **How did Jeremiah describe Zedekiah's situation (38:22 cf 38:6)?** Stuck in the mud! Jeremiah had experienced being physically stuck in the mud not that long ago. Jeremiah was sinking further and further down. He was hopeless in saving himself and the design was his death. It took 30 men to pull him out. But Zedekiah had no one come to his rescue as he was deserted by his trusted friends. *Your trusted friends have deceived you and prevailed against you… they turned away from you.* He was left in his helpless situation and the only thing he could do was to wait for the doom day to come.

As Jerusalem fell, we read the fate of King Zedekiah and his family (39:6-7). After witnessing the slaughter of his sons and nobles, his eyes were put out, condemning him to darkness for life just as he had been walking in spiritual darkness and refused the light of God's Word. Meanwhile, God's arm is never too short to preserve His faithful. Nebuchadnezzar singled Jeremiah out for favour, perhaps because he had heard of him speaking of Babylon's success. In the end the responsibility to take care of Jeremiah was passed down to Gedaliah, who was the son of Ahikam who had saved Jeremiah back in 26:24. Of course, Gedaliah's grandfather Shaphan served at Josiah's court. Ebed-melech, the Ethiopian eunuch who bravely saved Jeremiah from the mud, was spared too. He was commended for "trusting in God (v18)". God knows His own and individually. He is the Lord of Hosts, and His providence is manifested in the detailed plan for each individual.

Questions for reflection:

Although he was a son, he learned obedience through what he suffered. And being made perfect, he became the source of eternal salvation to all who obey him (Heb 5: 8-9). Obedience is not an easy lesson to learn in our faith walk and it is learnt through suffering. We see that in Ch. 32, Jeremiah obeyed God and purchased the land when he did not understand why. Today we have the example of the Rechabites.

What were the memorable lessons of obedience that God has taught you so far in your walk with Him? How has each episode changed your relationship with God? Has it become easier?

Which parts of God's teaching most trouble you in this session that you feel you can't submit right now? Would you submit them to God in prayer for the Spirit's enlightenment and lead?

SESSION TEN

Jeremiah 40-45

The bad figs: the fulfilment of (24:8-10 & 29:17-19)

Jeremiah's ministry spanned forty years leading up to the fall of Jerusalem. It is poignant to draw parallel with Moses who ministered to the people for forty years in the wilderness before they entered the Promised Land while Jeremiah ministered to them for 40 years before they went into exile from the Promised Land in the reverse direction.

We may think that the destruction of Jerusalem concluded his ministry as his prophecy had been largely fulfilled. He could retire from public ministry and live peacefully thereafter; didn't he deserve it? From his earlier lamentation of strife and contention (15:10), we know that this was his longing too. In fact, he had been set up nicely by the chief officials of Babylon to do that, so it seems. But as we see in this section of the text, it was not meant to be. Far from leading a peaceful life, Jeremiah witnessed brutal violence against his own by his own and how the perpetual sins of the small remnant paved their final demise as the prophesied bad figs.

I.   The remnant in Judah (Chs 40-41)

Note: the word that came to Jeremiah in 40:1 is picked up again from 42:7. In between these two verses, Jeremiah gave the setting of the occasion for the word given by God after 42:7. From 40:2, we see an expansion of 39:13-14.

How did the Babylonian captain of the guard understand their success in their military expedition against Judah (40:2-3)? Why is it astonishing? How do you think he came to this view? He bragged not of their own power or might but God's.   He attributed their success and Judah's disaster to God's doing and not theirs. He even cited the cause as the people's sin that brought this upon themselves. It is astonishing because he spoke with wisdom and understanding as God's people and not a gentile. He saw it all clearly even more so than the Jews themselves, who refused to acknowledge their sins and blame God for the ill-fate. How the captain came to this knowledge is hard to tell. Could he be listening to Jeremiah's preaching? Perhaps the utter destruction of the Jerusalem was indeed a military impossibility – the perfection of beauty and the joy of all the earth (Lam 2:15) with its impregnable natural defence (Ps 125:2) – that had been puzzling him. Otherwise how could a people that had been so favoured as they had been by the divine goodness would have been abandoned by God had they not be provoking?

Jeremiah had a real choice. What was it and what did his decision show about him (40:4-5)? Where was this conversation take place (40:1)? Somehow Jeremiah was bound up in chains and transported to Ramah (a small town five miles north of Jerusalem) where the captives were gathered, ready to be deported to Babylon. Jeremiah was soon distinguished.

Somehow he had earned the respect from Nebuzaradan the captain of the guard, who personally invited him to go to Babylon with him, not as a captive but as if his guest of honour for he promised to treat him well. This offer did not oblige Jeremiah, who was also given a free hand to choose to do what he thought right. Should he stay, he was advised to go to Gedaliah, no doubt because he was sure that Gedaliah would treat him well too. Jeremiah had been imprisoned during the siege by his own people for being God's prophet and now he was set free by his enemy, who seemed to be kinder to him and value him more than his own people. Jeremiah chose to stay in his homeland. He was not tempted by the promised comfort in a land that worshipped foreign gods. Rather, as all the elites had been rounded up, he might think that he would be useful to look after the weak and poor and vulnerable. His heart was still about service to his people even when they had been treating him treacherously. It was a pure heart of no hatred or self-interest.

The King of Babylon had appointed a Jew to be the governor of in the land rather than posting a Babylonian. This might be a gesture of goodwill. **What do we know about Gedaliah from the bible texts?** He was from a family of government administrators. His grandfather Shaphan served in Josiah's court and was involved in his reforms. His father Ahikam was also an official. He saved Jeremiah from the hands of the officials and the religious elites who wanted to put him to death. His uncles Gemariah also served in Jehoiakim's court (36:12). His family pedigree was such that he was likely to be a competent government administrator. When entrusted with the task, he did not seem daunted. Rather, he seemed to be full of confidence to restart life there. He was definitely not bloodthirsty but a peacemaker. With a heart eager to do good for the people, one could say he was naïve about court politics. He refused to think ill of people when he declined the offer of Johanan to kill Ishmael who was believed to be plotting against him. He appeared to be someone known and commanded confidence as the Judeans who had been scattered across the country were willing to come to him on hearing that he was made governor. He definitely had the confidence of the king of Babylon. **What was his governing principle (40:9-10 cf 39:10)?** The poor were given vineyards and fields but they did not own them. They were to serve the king of Babylon. Yet Gedaliah reassured them that they need not be afraid. He would deal with the Chaldeans on their behalf, so that they could focus on enjoying the produce of the land. And indeed they gathered in great abundance (40: 12). All signs pointed to a promising start. **Why do you think Ishmael was conspiring against Gedaliah (hint 41:1)?** Ishmael was a royal seed. Could he be jealous of Gedaliah for his popularity and commissioned power from the king of Babylon?

The massacre he subsequently committed against the worshippers bringing with them grain offerings and incense showed an uncontrollable rage which seemed disproportionate if he just wished to displace Gedaliah. Could he be provoked by their loyalty to Gedaliah as they clearly trusted him? Or did he simply hate those who were critical of him by their actions? Ten were spared not for his love of mercy but his love of money. He threw the dead bodies into the large cistern that King Asa had made for defence against Baasha king of Israel. (For background, read 1 Kings 15:16-22.) What was intended to defend his people was then used as a common grave of the people. In so doing, he denied them honour and dignity of a proper burial. Ishmael was barbaric in all his actions. He took everyone captive in Mizpah to the Ammonites. Among them were the king's daughters. Johanan and all the leaders of the forces with him came to their rescue. The captives seemed happy to return when a new leader emerged. They all turned back but Johanan let Ishmael and his men escape and did not pursue them.

What reason did the remnant under the leadership of Johanan cite for their intention to go to Egypt (41: 17-18)? They said that they were afraid of the Chaldeans as their appointed governor had been murdered. It does not seem to be a sound reason because they were not responsible for Gedaliah's death. It should be Ishmael who should have been afraid. Nonetheless, they seemed convinced that Egypt was the only safe place to escape from the Chaldeans. Their jittering may be understandable. After all it was a land that had been through horrendous disaster. Just as they tried to restart, Ishmael and his men made them relive the horror. They may wonder if the land was cursed, if it was safe, if they could ever have peace there. At that crossroad, they came to Jeremiah.

II.   Obstinate disobedience exposed (Chs. 42-44)

Should God go ahead and wipe out the remnant in Judah, we may exclaim, "This is unjust; what have they done?" God has already said previously:

In vain have I struck your children; they took no correction (2:30).
O LORD, do not your eyes look for truth? You have stuck them down but they felt no anguish; you have consumed them, but they refused to take correction. They have made their faces harder than rock; they have refused to repent (5:3).
'This is the nation that did not obey the voice of the LORD their God, and did not accept discipline (7:28).'

God makes what is invisible to us but known to Him visible and known to us so that we don't doubt His justice. God let the events unfold to expose the nature of the Jews' disobedience, which makes the obedience of Rechabites to Jonadah even more remarkable in contrast. We must admire God's patience in persistently engaging with this stiff-necked people.

If we listen only to their plea to Jeremiah in 42:1-6, what would

we conclude about the people? "Finally they have listened! Finally they have turned back from their ways!" They pleaded mercy of God, for they were only few left. They sought direction in their life when they were lost. They promised universal obedience that *whether it is good or bad, we will obey the voice of the* LORD *our God... that it may be well with us* (42:6). They were pitch-perfect in religious language. **What did Jeremiah promise to do in return (42:4)?** He will give the whole counsel of God to them; he will not hold back anything from them.

God did not give an instant answer. **When the word finally came after ten days, what was God's message to the remnant that they should do (42: 7-12)?** God instructed them to remain in the land; then he will build them up and not pull them down; he will plant them and not pluck them up. He also addressed their specific concern about the Chaldeans. God promises that He will save them, deliver them and be with them, so they do not need to be afraid. **What was the warning if they disobeyed God's voice (42: 13-18)?** Going back to Egypt was a curse of disobedience (see Deut 28:68). The people were unwittingly wishing a curse on themselves! They did not believe in God but in their ability to dodge their fate. They believed that by escaping to Egypt, they could escape God's judgement. In reply, God told them that judgement will follow them no matter where they run to. They will be pursued by the sword, famine and pestilence, the same fate as Jerusalem under siege. All will die; there will be no survivor. The worst fate they so desperately wish to avoid will follow them. Once they were a great nation of God's favour and blessings to all the nations of the earth, they shall become an execration, a horror, a curse and a taunt (42:18). **What was Jeremiah's counsel to them (42:19-22)?** Before we inquire God, there may be uncertainty. Once God has spoken, we can *know for a certainty* (v19): Do not go to Egypt or you have gone astray at the cost of your lives (v20). If the past record was anything to go by, Jeremiah did not harboured high hope because "you have not obeyed the voice of the LORD your God in anything that he sent me to tell you" (v21). Know for a certainty that you will die if you leave this land.

What was the people's reaction to God's message (43:2-3)? When God's message is found contradicting to our opinion, God is wrong! They charged Jeremiah of lying. They claimed it as a trap to hand them over to the Chaldeans and send them into exile. This pride in us God needs to humble or we can never have listening ears and hearts to God's Word. **Given this response, how do we interpret what they say in 42:1-6?** Their pitch perfect speech before God made their disobedience inexcusable and wilful as they knew full well what was expected of them. They had made up their mind to go to Egypt notwithstanding. They wanted to fake obedience and oblige God's favour should God's will so happen echo their mind as if God could be cheated on. We do not truly desire to know the mind of God if we do not fully resolve to comply with it when we do know it. <u>Obedience of convenience is no obedience at all.</u> The Judeans' obstinate disobedience was clearly exposed. They professed one thing and intended another, promising what they never meant to perform; the wicked are inconsistent with themselves. They had the disposition to disobey. It boiled down to that fact that they did not trust in God and their fear loomed larger than God.

The leaders took <u>all</u> the remnant of Judah to Egypt, including Jeremiah and Baruch to go with them. **Where did they settle (43:8-9)?** Tahpanhes was a famous city in Egypt, which was named after a queen (1 Kings 11:19). That city housed Pharaoh's palace, which can be a residence owned by Pharaoh or a government building. In other words, they settled in a place close to the heart of the nation. **What was Jeremiah's prophecy there (43:8-13)?** Jeremiah set large stones in the pavement near Pharaoh's palace, to make known to the people that the

Chaldeans were coming and Nebuchadnezzar, whom God calls "His servant", would set up his royal throne on the exact spot as marked out. The message to the Judeans was clear: their effort to evade the grasp of the Chaldeans was futile. God's Word defines our reality, not our perceived circumstances.

There had been more Judeans living in Egypt than the group just arrived from Jerusalem under the leadership of Johanan and others. Jeremiah ministered to them like when he was in Jerusalem. **How did they live that provoked God (44:7-10)?** Just like Judah did not learn the lesson of Israel, the remnant from Judah in Egypt had failed to learn the lesson from what had happened to Judah and Jerusalem. They provoked God with the works of their hands as they made offerings to the foreign gods of Egypt. Sin is self-destructive as expressed in v7: *Why do you commit this great evil against yourselves, to cut off from you man and woman, infant and child, from the midst of Judah, leaving you no remnant? ... so that you become a curse and a taunt among the nations of the earth (v8)?* **What did God pronounce that He would do (44:13-14)?** God pronounces that they will face the same punishment as those in Jerusalem, with the sword, famine and pestilence which they have tried to evade, and they will be wiped out, except some fugitives.

Those who live in disobedience to God commonly grow worse and worse, and the heart is more and more hardened by the deceitfulness of sin. **How did the people justify their practice (44:15-18)?** (1) What they did was nothing new as they followed only their fathers' footsteps. (2) Those in authority, like their kings and officials, did the same. (3) It was done out in the open *in the streets.* (4) It was a practice that a great multitude did in unison too: *all the people who lived in Pathros.* (5) Then they enjoyed prosperity. They reasoned that the disasters that had struck them as the wrath of the queen of heaven over their slacking off in making offerings and pouring out drink offerings to her. To protect themselves and wish for good fortunes, their allegiance was with the queen of heaven. They openly declared that they would not listen to Jeremiah (44:16). **How did Jeremiah answer to that (44:23)?** It is their sin and disobedience that this disaster has happened to them. Sin is their own enemy; through sinning, they are their own murderers. It seems Nebuzaradan the captain of the guard had more divine understanding than the Judeans (40:2-3). **How would you summarise God's final judgement on the Judeans (44:24-30)?** (1) As they have requested, God gives them up to their own depraved practice. On this side of heaven, no judgement is worse than being given up in the lusts of our hearts to impurity. (2) He disowns them – His name will not be invoked by the mouth of any man of Judah in all the land of Egypt. God's "name" is not just a label but His being. It means that they will not know God anymore. God throws them into the darkness of the heathens who have no light of God. (3) From now on, He is set for their harm. (4) This is for His name's sake, so that they know whose word will stand, His or theirs. (5) Same fate as what they have tried to evade awaits them.

We hear no more of these Judeans in Egypt from the sacred history. God's Word is final; do we need to hear any more? This is the chilling end of the bad figs in terms of their relationship with God. In 586/7 BC Nebuchadnezzar led a campaign against Egypt as Jeremiah had foretold, 18/19 years after the fall of Jerusalem.

III. Message to Baruch (Ch. 45)

The time marker goes back to the fourth year of Jehoiakim, which was the year of the first deportation, the beginning of the end for Jerusalem.

What was the impact of working with Jeremiah on Baruch (45:3)? Baruch was not a prophet but Jeremiah's scribe, probably a scholar. Still through his work with the prophet, he shared the burden of foresight and it was weighing on him. He was young and seeking out to do great things for himself. Yet the prophecy was just grim, grim, and more grim. How does a youngster face with the prophecy of no future? It is hard to believe that the world order that you know is going to be no more and their home is going to be destroyed. There is nowhere for anyone to gain a footing. He was sorrowful, groaning and found no rest. **What was God's counsel to him (45:4-5)?** He confirms His intention and the destruction will be total. All that we see before our eyes are uncertain and perishing. Therefore it is better for Baruch not be too attached to this world or have too high expectations of it. God's agenda reigns supreme and not his personal one; his outlook of life needs to change. God promises to preserve him. Life is great mercy and favour in the midst of dense flying arrows of death. His goal of life is not for his personal glory but God's glory.

Questions for reflection:

Have you ever been "seeking great things for yourself" (45:5)? What does God say to you in that endeavour?

Is there any area where you struggle with obedience to God? How have you been debating with God on the subject? How would you move forward?

What is your reality: God's Word or your perceived circumstances?

SESSION ELEVEN

Jeremiah 46-49

God of all nations

In this section of the prophecy, we see 25:15-26 spelt out in details, pronouncing God's judgement on each of the powers. The king of Babylon was to be used by God as the instrument to execute His judgement on them. It therefore foretold at the same time that Babylon would prevail over "all the nations" for a period but thereafter, Babylon itself would be judged (Chs. 50 & 51).

Israel was surrounded by enemies on all sides in her history and the OT records many wars with them. The expectation of judgement on Israel's enemies permeates the Psalter. For examples:

Ps 6: 1: *All my enemies shall be ashamed and greatly troubled; they shall turn back and be put to shame in a moment.*
Ps 7: 6: *Arise, O LORD, in your anger; lift yourself up against the fury of my enemies; awake for me; you have appointed a judgement.*
Ps 54: 5, 7: *He will return the evil to my enemies; in your faithfulness put an end to them...For he has delivered me from every trouble, and*

my eye has looked in triumph on my enemies.

Ps 89: 50-51: *Remember, O Lord, how your servants are mocked, and how I bear in my heart the insults of all the many nations, with which your enemies mock, O LORD, with which they mock the footsteps of your anointed.*

Ps 97: 8: *Zion hears and is glad, and the daughters of Judah rejoice, because of your judgements, O LORD.*

Having judged the household of God, the remaining chapters of Jeremiah (except Ch. 52) lays out God's judgement on the enemies of His people. Both Isaiah and Ezekiel prophesied against these nations that Jeremiah is prophesying here, and with reference to the same events.

I.   Judgement on Egypt (Ch. 46)

Following Chs. 43 and 44, judgement on Egypt comes first of the list. **What was the relationship between Egypt and Israel in the history of OT (Deut 17: 16, 1 Sam 12:8, Is 31:1&3)?** Egypt was a great power in the antiquity. They were an age old oppressor of Israel, from whom God had delivered them. Egypt had seen the great wonders of God during the Exodus: the ten plagues and the parting of the Red Sea. During Exodus was a great cluster of miracles so that "they shall know that I am the LORD their God" (Ex 29:46). If seeing miracles would make someone believe, Egypt should have no excuse for their unbelief. God specifically commanded His people not to return to Egypt (Deut 17:16). Yet Israel often trusted in Egypt for help, in their horses and chariots, which were many with their strong horsemen. This offended God as they did not look to God or consult Him but trust in man instead (Is 31:1). We have also seen in the previous chapters that the remnant of Jerusalem rated Egypt a safer haven than God's protection. Deceived by this false sense of security, they were determined to go to Egypt against God's command and took refuge there.

When Babylon was rising to be a force to be reckoned with, Judah became a buffer state between these two great powers. 46:2 records an encounter at Carchemish between them in the fourth year of Jehoiakim. **What was the outcome of this encounter (46:2 cf 2 Kings 24:7)?** Nebuchadnezzar defeated Pharaoh Neco, thereby recovering from the river of Egypt to the river of Euphrates, all that belonged to Egypt. Egypt was so weakened that he did not come again any more out of his land. That is, it brought to a close Egypt's political and military influence over Palestine and Syria. **Four years prior, whom did Pharaoh Neco slay (2 Kings 23:28-29)?** He killed Josiah in the battle and God made him pay dearly in his defeat at Carchemish.

46:3-12 describes the battle at Carchemish. **What was their confidence war cry?** The preparation of the army for war was impressive. All the equipment and horses were set up and ready (v3-4) and showed specialisation of the force (v9). They were eager to go to war and their vision was grand. They believed that they would rise like River Nile and cover the earth (v8). They were fighting to enlarge themselves and for dignity. **What were they like during engagement (v5)?** Cowardice gripped them – they were dismayed and the mighty warriors fled a fight in haste; they were terrified. **Why (v10)?** *Many are the plans in the mind of a man, but it is the purposes of the LORD that will stand* (Prov 19:21). Pharaoh meant it for their prestige and enlargement, but God meant it for the great humiliation and weakening of their kingdom in vengeance on the foes of His people. All the preparation for a victorious encounter came to nothing but in vain when God fights against them.

> **Gilead** is situated east of Jordan River. It is a fertile land. The tribes of Reuben and Gad did not want to cross the river once they arrived there (Num 32). Moses granted the land to these two tribes and half a tribe of Manasseh. Rising from the Jordan Valley on the west, 700 ft below sea level, Gilead rises to heights of more than 3000ft. It is a well-watered hill country, thickly wooded. It is known for its grapes, olives, fruit trees, and pasture lands. The "balm of Gilead" referred to an ointment with medicinal value.

What was the outcome of Egypt healing herself (46:11-12)? Even when they had the best medicine the land could offer at the time, in vain they applied them as there was no healing of the nation or halting of their decline.

After their previous campaign "out of their land", they were made disabled to make any attempts on other nations. The rest of the oracle foretold that Nebuchadnezzar was coming to them and they met the smiting on their own soil (46:13)! Nebuchadnezzar invaded Egypt in 568-567BC. Unlike 46:3, the preparation called in v14 was for defence and not for offence. **What is special about the place names in 46:14 (cf 44:1)?** The call must have been made in all parts of Egypt but particularly in Migdol, Memphis and Tahpanhes where the Jewish refugees or fugitives had planted themselves in contempt of God's command. **Did they stand a chance against the invader (46:15, 21-23, 25)?** They did not stand a chance because God intended to thrust them down. The appointed time was marked as their day of calamity, the time of their punishment. The Egyptians were no more able to resist the attack than the tree was to resist the man who came with an axe to cut it down. Soldiers deserted their posts and those willing to fight had no reinforcement. All arose and turned back. Egypt was such a populous and rich country with many hidden treasures. They would plunder the land like locusts without number, leaving widespread destruction and devastation after they had passed (v19). The instrument God used was once again *the hand of a people from the north* (v24). **What was the name of Pharaoh reduced to (46:17 cf 46:7-8; Is 2:11)?** All his big and mighty talk came to nothing but a noise which brought nothing to pass at the promised time. His credibility was ruined and this did not build people's confidence.

Who was God speaking to in v27-28 and why? What has the judgement on Egypt got to do with *Jacob*? This is an encouragement to God's people. Remember they were in exile and wondered what would become of them or the world. God is reassuring His people that in time of turmoil, His promise to them is not swayed. He reiterates their promised restoration and their return to home, where they will have quiet and ease. God knows they are afraid but He says to them, fear not "for I am with you." Notice that God is treating His own and other people differently: *I will make a full end of all the nations, but of you I will not make a full end.* To His people, His "punishment" is really fatherly *discipline in just measure.* 1 Peter 4:17: *For it is time for judgement to begin at the household of God; and if it begins with us, what will be the outcome for those who do not obey the gospel of God?* Ultimately to truly deliver His people from slavery and to grant them lasting rest, the enemies of His people need to be conquered and defeated once and for all. The rescue story of His people will not be complete if the enemies are not squashed and come to a full end in one way or another.

II.   Judgement on the Philistine (Ch. 47)

Israel had many battles against **the Philistines**. The famous ones were the story of Samson in Judg 13:1-7 and David against Goliath in 1 Sam 17: 1-58. "As the Egyptians had often proved false friends, so the Philistines had always been sworn enemies, to the Israel of God, and the more dangerous and vexatious for their being such near neighbours to them. They were considerably humbled in David's time, but, it seems they had got head again and were a considerable people till Nebuchadnezzar cut them off with their neighbours, which is the event here foretold" (from Matthew Henry's commentary).

The date of this prophecy is noted: it was *before Pharaoh struck down Gaza* (47:1). "The Egyptians attacked the Philistines on several occasions, including an assault before the Battle Megiddo in 609 BC [where King Josiah was killed] and also in 601 BC. Yet the Philistines' downfall will not come at the hands of the Egyptians but rather the Babylonians, the 'waters rising out of the north' (v2)" (from Reformation Study Bible). That is, the prophecy came at a time when the Philistines were in their full strength and lustre and were not in peril or under threats.

What does *waters* represent in Hebrew writings (Rev 17:15 and Ps 69)? Waters signify multitudes of people and nations in Rev as well as great and threatening calamities in OT. Here they signify both. **How was the force of invasion described?** The strength of Babylonian army was consistent. Their power was overwhelming that the Chaldean army was to overflow the land like a deluge. The rumbling of their massive army of horses and chariots was threatening and frightening. **What was the response of the Philistines?** The men had no heart to fight but cried and wailed like children. They were fleeing in such a fright that parents did not look back to their children. Their hands were feeble to carry the burden of others' safety even for their own children. **How long would it last?** The prophet expressed an earnest desire to see the end of war (v6). But the biblical truth

is that the sword of war has its charge from the Lord of hosts.
Every bullet is directed by the all-seeing God rather than blind.
It will last as long as it is appointed to fulfil its charge.

III. Judgement on Moab (Ch. 48)

> **Moabites** and Ammonites were descendants of Lot with his two
> daughters after the destruction of Sodom and Gomorrah (see Gen 19: 24-
> 38). "Moab was Israel's enemy (Judg 3:12-14; 2 Kings 3:4-27). It was an
> ally of Judah against Babylon (27:3), but supplied troops for
> Nebuchadnezzar against Jehoiakim (2 Kings 24:2). Its defeat by
> Nebuchadnezzar may have come in 582 BC after a rebellion."
>
> "Nebo ... Kiriathaim (v1) were towns originally allocated to the tribe of
> Reuben (Num 32:3, 37, 38; Josh 13:15, 19). Since they are in the northern
> part of Moab, they will be overrun first in a Babylonian invasion" (from
> the Reformation Study Bible). Heshbon (v2) was a principle city of
> Moab, also assigned to Reuben (Num 32:37; Josh 13:17).

Who was the author of Moab's destruction (48:1, 10)? The Lord
of the hosts. It was the work of God. God again sent one as His
instrument. **How was the sent instrument expected to
discharge his duty (48:10) and what would have happened if he
slacked (1 Sam 15:2-3, 7-11, 26)?** *Cursed is he who does the work of
the LORD with slackness* and in this case, the work of God was not
to keep back His sword from bloodshed. There was a similar
case with Saul who was sent to strike the Amalekites. God
instructed Saul to devote to destruction and spare no one. Yet
Saul did not fulfil this charge of the attack but spare King Agag
and the best of the livestock. God rejected him as king. **When
was the charge against Moab fulfilled (48:2, 8, 9)?** It was
fulfilled when the renown of Moab was no more. The madman
was silenced. They were to inflict on them desolation and great
destruction with no inhabitant. It was comprehensive as the
destroyer would come on every city and no city was to escape.
There was an urgency to flee (v6). **What was Moab guilty of**

(48:7, 11-13, 26, 29-30, 35)? They trusted in their works and treasures. Moab was an ancient kingdom before Israel was, and had enjoyed great peace – *Moab has been at ease from his youth and has settled on his dregs* (v11). They had never been poured out or taken into captivity. However, this prosperity had worked against them as their hearts and lives were unchanged, i.e. a wicked idolatrous nation. They put confidence in the false god that they worshipped called Chemosh, and they should be ashamed just as Israel was ashamed of Bethel, where Israel performed Golden Calf take two. They projected themselves in their idol worship, as idol worship often does, so they magnified themselves against God. Their pride was unbearable to God who also hates boastful tongue.

What were the parallels between Moab's Chemosh and Israel's Bethel (48:13)? Read 1 Kings 12:25-33. It was the second incident of Golden Calves in the history of Israel. Jeroboam took control of the northern kingdom called Ephraim or Israel. Jeroboam was concerned that if the people had to always go up to Jerusalem for their religion, they would be attached to Jerusalem and their loyalty would be turned back to the king of Judah. Jeroboam's solution to this problem was to fabricate a counterfeit religious system for his people to keep them away from Jerusalem. He made not one but two golden calves to be placed in Bethal and Dan respectively. He built temple and appointed his own priests who were not Levites. He appointed his own religious calendar and religious practices. Jeroboam himself went up to Bethal to worship his golden calf. Moab committed the same folly as Israel: Those who will not be convicted and made ashamed of the folly of their idolatry by the word of God shall be convicted and made ashamed of it by the judgements of God, when they learn that they have put their confidence into something utterly useless.

How was the attack described? It was sudden and swift (v16, 40). The ruin was extensive and comprehensive (v15, 20, 34, 41-42). Their power was snapped totally (v25) and their warriors lost their valour (v17, 41). Joy deserted them and in its place was wailing (v33, 36, 37-39). Judgement would pursue them wherever they went (v43-44). **Yet was this Moab's final chapter (48:47)?** God has promised to restore the fortunes of Moab in the latter days. Judgement on Moab went no further.

IV. Judgement on other nations (Ch. 49)

Ammonites were descendants of Lot and therefore were kindred to Moabites, who were also neighbours. Ammon was situated on the east side of Jordan River and shared borders with the two and a half tribes in the northern kingdom. When Assyria came to take the northern kingdom into captive, the territories in Gilead were left dispeopled and unguarded (2 Kings 15:29; 1 Chron 5:26).

What had God against the Ammonites (49:1 cf Amos 1:13; Zeph 2:8)? God charged them of illegal encroachment upon the right possessions of the tribe of Gad which lay next to them geographically. There were more rightful heirs to the territories than the Ammonites. Moreover, God knew their act of violence of killing rightful heirs by ripping open pregnant women in order to enlarge their border (Amos 1:13). They did it to "taunt God's people and make boast of their territory" (Zeph 2:8). God set out to right the wrong that *Israel shall dispossess those who dispossessed them* (v2).

Application: What do we learn about God's view on private ownership? Some use the Bible to argue for common ownership. No, God supports private ownership or there will be no "thou shall not steal" in the Ten Commandments. The Mosaic Law covered inheritance and we see it acted out in Ch. 32 with Jeremiah being asked to exercise his right of possession and redemption over a field (32:8) within his family. Those who think everything they can lay hands on as their own are mistaken. As there is justice owing to owners and to their heirs, it is a great sin to defraud them. Even if the injured parties may not know about their right or how it has come about, God holds out justice for them.

How was God to judge them (49:3-5)? He brought down terror on them, and exiled their idol (Milcom) with his priests and officials. They were called *faithless* because as descendants of righteous Lot, they trusted in her treasures which they thought would protect them. God drove them out of their land. **Was this the end for them (49:6)?** No, God promises to restore them.

> **Edom** was the other name for Esau (Gen 25:30), who was the father of Edomites with his Canaanite wives (Gen 36:: 1-2, 9). Jacob, the father of Israelites, was Esau's twin brother. As such, Edomites and Judah were of the same blood. Esau was Jacob's estranged brother, and Edom was an old enemy to Israel. Teman and Dedan represented the northern and southern limits of Edom; Bozrah was the capital of Edom.

What was Edom punished for (49:7,16, Obadiah 10-14, Ps 137:7)? They were proud in their wisdom with their statesmen excelling in politics, and their seemingly impregnable natural defence. God was to take them all down to humble them. When they gloated over the misfortune of Judah and helped ransacked Jerusalem, it was particularly bitter. If holy men were caught up in the calamity of Judah, could they expect to be left unpunished and not drink the cup of judgement (v12)? **Who was the instrument of judgement sent (49:19 cf 4:7 and 49:22 cf 48:40)?** Nebuchadnezzar but the Edomites were also conquered decisively by the Arabs during 6th century BC. **What would their calamity be like?** The stripping of Esau would see no leniency as grape-gatherers or thieves would (v9-10). It would be stripped bare and nothing could be concealed. Edom would become a horror, a taunt, a waste and a curse among the nations (v13, 17) instead of a nation with pride. The courage of the warriors would fail them (v22) as they reckoned how formidable their enemy was. But there was one comfort which is in v11: *Leave* *your fatherless children; I will keep them alive; and let your widows trust in me.*

Elam was an important power to the east of Babylon. The prophecy possibly relates to a Babylonian containment campaign against Elam in 595BC. This prophecy is specifically dated to the beginning of Zedekiah's reign (597BC). That means it was before the fall of Jerusalem and Judah. The strength of Elam might have offered hope to Judah that they could counterbalance the threat of Babylon and turned the situation in their favour. Elam was famous for its archers. They had acted against God's Israel before (see Is 22:6). God typically breaks us on our strength, so that what we have trusted most is first to fail us. The prophecy therefore opens with "Behold, I will break the bow of Elam, the mainstay of their might (v35)." God would stir up powers from all parts of the world to be against Elam, the people of which would be scattered with them. They would be terrified. God Himself would set His throne in Elam (v38), showing His sovereign rule over nations. Again, this was not the end of Elam (v39). Indeed we see them turn up in Acts 2:9, among those at the Pentecost and speaking in tongues. What return can be more desirable than being set free by Christ?

Damascus was the metropolis of the kingdom of Syria, lying north of Canaan. Hamath and Arpad (v23) were two major city states. Ben-hadad (v27) was not a personal name but a title like Pharaoh for the king of Egypt. It identified the ruler of Syria as the son of the god Hadad.

How quickly our confidence and courage melt away and panic grips us, when the troubled sea drowns us in fear. Anguish and sorrow replaces the joy we used to have. A city of praise never stands on her own merits. However splendid and strong it once was, it can crumble and fall in no time. How fleeting is world glamour which offers no guarantee of the future?

> **Kedar** descended from Ishmael (Gen 25:13). They were one of the Arab settlements. They were known as "the people of the east" (v28). Arab tribes were nomadic and could pose periodic threat to settled communities in the ancient world (e.g. Judg 6:1-6). "The present prophecy may be occasioned by an Arab uprising against Nebuchadnezzar in 598 BC. They have few cities, so the judgement is aimed at the markers of wealth in their community – tents, flocks and camels" (from Reformation Study Bible). Nonetheless, they were wealthy, self-sufficient nations, that their lives were easy, dwelt securely without gates or bars, and they dwelt alone. When Nebuchadnezzar struck them, they cried out, "Terror on every side (v29)!"

Questions for meditation:

Do you rejoice in God's judgement? Why? Is Ps 58:10-11 hard to contemplate?

In what do you place your confidence?

What does the study teach you about the character of God? How does the knowledge of God strengthen your faith in your situation?

SESSION TWELVE

Jeremiah 50-52

I.   Judgement on Babylon (Chs. 50-51)

In what sense the prophecy against Babylon is the climax of the book (hint: Ps 137)? To God's people, the shadow of Babylon has loomed large throughout the whole book as a mighty menacing enemy preying on them. She represents a formidable enemy that God's people cannot overcome. Instead their nightmare has come true – they are humiliated in the utter defeat of their nation with everything that was once their joy and pride destroyed. The focal point of their religious life and identity is flattened and they must have felt the presence of God departed from them. They are taken away as captives and live in subjugation to an unholy people who don't know their God. Psalm 137 expresses their sentiments in exile that there is no song of joy and they cannot and do not allow themselves to forget Jerusalem. Even though restoration of God's people has been promised in the prophecy, the victory is not complete or reassuring if the archenemy is not destroyed to repay what they have done to Judah. How can Judah rest in peace if Babylon is around? The previous prophecies in Chs. 46-49 against Israel's enemies have served to affirm that Babylon will be a world

105

power for a period and act as the appointed instrument of God's wrath up to a point. It is important that the book of Jeremiah concludes with the judgement on Babylon as their final enemy. It comes last in the book because it is the last to accomplish among the others.

The fall of Babylon is foretold again in Rev 18. What has Babylon come to symbolise in the Bible (Gen 11:1-9 & Is 13:1-22, esp v11)? *Babylon* is the Latin representation of the Greek name derived from its native name meaning "the gate of gods". Its Hebrew name is Babel, meaning "confusion". The tower of Babel is the corporate human effort to create a city that will define their existence independent of God and in turn to stand in opposition to God. It was in the land of Shinar, which was where Nebuchadnezzar's Babylon was based (Dan 1:2). In Isaiah 13-14, the description of Babylon and its king transcends the earthly kingdom of the Chaldeans and represents all the kingdoms of this world in rebellion against God. In Rev, it comes to represent the coalition of Satan and the kingdoms of this world that opposes Christ and His Church. While Babylon was the enemy to Judah in history, the judgement of Babylon has a spiritual dimension that points to the apocalyptic triumphs of the gospel church in the latter days over the NT Babylon. Recall in 23:7-8, Jeremiah prophesies that the pluck up of the house of Judah from the north country will eclipse their exodus from Egypt in greatness. That rescue involves the destruction of Babylon that goes beyond the earthly powers, typifying the gospel triumphs of all believers over the power of darkness; the fall of Babylon is the end of all that opposes the Lord's rule.

What was the date of this prophecy (51:59)? It was in the early reign of Zedekiah, meaning that it was before the destruction of Jerusalem and the final deportation of the Jews. That is, Jeremiah was prophesying the doom of Babylon when it was a rapidly rising power, characterised by its swiftness in attack, military might and mercilessness. **Against this background, how would 50:2 read to the original audience?** (1) It was a public broadcast, and not to a private audience as it were. It was not to be concealed but to be known among the nations. This is gutsy. This confidence did not derive from the political assessment of the day but shows that Jeremiah was very sure of where his authority came from, so he thundered it as from heaven. (2) The tone of the prophecy is certainty – Babylon is taken! Bel, their idol, is put to shame and Merodach, possibly their venerable king during Hezekiah's reign in Judah, is dismayed. Babylon's confidence, anchored in the help of their idol, their wealth and their renowned military prowess, was vain and empty before God. It was so certain that it was proclaimed as already done! Looking back to Ch. 40, why the king of Babylon was kind to Jeremiah when they took Jerusalem was God's grace! **Application: do you have an eternal vision rooted in the Bible which looks incredible from an earthly perspective? What does this faith in God's word look like in your daily life and impact on your mental strength?**

The appointed instrument was "out of the north" also. They were the Persians and the Medes (51:11). **To whom do verses 4-10 & 17-20 address?** God's people. **What is the message?**

50:4-5, 18-20: The path to their restoration is repentance and reconciliation with God. Here they display godly sorrow with a mixture of tears of repentance for sin and tears of joy for the goodness of God in their deliverance. Godly sorrow leads them to seek God and sorrow soon turns to joy. What action does repentance produce (v5)? Remember "the ancient path" in 6:16 and God's counsel in 31:21: *Set up road markers for yourself; make yourself guideposts; consider well the highway, the road by which you went. Return, O virgin Israel, return to these your cities.* With Babylon subdued, where is the heart longing of God's people? Back to Zion. They will be restored to the blessed land where they will experience abundance and fruitfulness of the land and their desire satisfied. Having been judged for breaking the covenant and repented, they should now cherish the covenantal relationship with God. God graciously paves the way for the remnants to renew the covenant that cannot be broken or forgotten. Sins have caused the separation between God and His people. Therefore in the solution, sins will not be found among His people not because they become perfect but because God forgives their sins (v20). And this is only possible through the work of Christ.

50:6-7, 17: The people in exile are lamentable. God still has them engraved in His heart. Banished from the presence of God, the people are vulnerable to the malice of their oppressors; they are lost sheep and hunted sheep. Their enemies think that they have a licence to be cruel to God's people for their sins but God will judge their wickedness.

50:8-10: Their life as exiles is sad but it is not going to be forever. God will open a path for them to *flee from the midst of Babylon, and go out of the land of the Chaldeans.* The male goats possess more boldness than sheep, and they go before the flock because no fear restrains them. It intimates that God will take away every fear of danger from the Jews who can go freely without the worry of being punished by the Chaldeans because they will be ruined. The arrows are ready and are aimed at God's enemies. When God gives commission he will give success. As they have plundered Judah, they will be plundered till nothing is left and *all who plunder her shall be sated* (v10).

What is the fate of Babylon and for what is Babylon punished (50:11-16, 21-29, 38)? She has sinned against God (v14) and opposed Him (v24). *For it is a land of images, and they are mad over idols* (v38). She faces God's wrath (v13), *for this is the vengeance of the LORD: take vengeance on her; do to her as she has done* (v15, also v29). The vengeance is for His temple (v28). *She has proudly defied the LORD, the Holy One of Israel* (v29) and *the proud one shall* *stumble and fall, with none to raise him up* (v32). Her fate is turned round: *How the hammer of the whole earth is cut down and broken* and become a horror among nations (v23). She will be plundered as how she has plundered others and made herself fat (v11). She will be disgraced and shamed, turned into a wilderness, a dry land and a desert. The land shall not be inhabited in utter desolation. She is attacked and won't stand. Her wounds are so bad that they are hissed at. God has set up against them (v25). At an appointed time, judgement will fall on her (v27).

50:33-34 are key verses. What memory does the wording deliberately evoke? Exodus from Egypt. Jeremiah often draws parallels between the two. **What was the state that God's people find themselves in (v33)?** Israel as the northern kingdom of ten tribes was sent into exile and destroyed by Assyria 136 years before Judah was taken into captivity by Babylon. It is suggested that the remnants of the ten tribes and the new captives of the two tribes might have mingled together upon Babylon taking over Assyria, and were united in their fate once more. They were held against their will under a cruel tyranny, which held them fast and refused to let them go. Sound very similar, doesn't it? They were in a situation of despair because they found themselves weak and helpless, who could save them? **What was the comforting message (v34)?** We have a Redeemer stronger than our adversary, and the LORD of hosts is his name. He is greater than all (John 10:29). He can overpower all enemies. The important thing is that He is on our side! *He will surely plead their cause.* Their restlessness will find rest in Him at last. Their fortune and that of Babylon will be reversed. **What does the message symbolise also?** We are enslaved by our sin. Its dominion holds us fast and we find ourselves weak under its hold. But our Redeemer is stronger and He is our advocate. The strength needed to pluck us up from among the land of slavery is significant because of the resistance – they hold the captives fast. But it will be overpowered and rest is promised to His people.

What is a sign that God is not on your side (50:43; 51:30)? In place of valour, they become weak, confused, helpless, anxious, totally disarmed and experiencing pain as of a woman in labour, i.e. not in a state to fight against anyone. **Describe the character of the One who has taken on Babylon (50:44-46).** All these will happen to the hammer of the world because God is mightier and He is sovereign over all. He is the only one who can do whatever He pleases. None is like Him nor can anyone stand before Him. His mind and will are set against Babylon, so it shall be. The fall of Babylon was a significant event in the world (the earth shall tremble) as well as in the spiritual realm (v46).

Ch. 51 is another lengthy section on the judgement on Babylon. **What does it suggest when Jeremiah expenses so many words on the downfall of Babylon?** It is an event hardly credible. The world regarded the Babylonians as half gods; the power of the Babylonian monarchy filled the minds of men with astonishment (50:46; 51:29). The length, the details, the repetitions and the many reasons are for emphasis and persuasion of a people in distress and find it hard to hold onto hope.

51:5: what sets apart Israel and Judah on the one hand and the Chaldeans on the other? Their difference is not that one is guilty and the other is not. We know both have sinned against God. The difference lies in that the former is God's covenant people whom God will never forsake. Recall the scandalous love God has for His wayward wife back in Ch. 3. **How is Babylon described (51:7-9 cf Rev 17:1-6)?** Babylon is a golden cup in God's hand which He has filled with treasures and blessings (abominations), which make all the earth drunken in their excesses as well as the terror she inflicts. Suddenly their accustomed way of life is broken down and chaos ensues. There are attempts to heal her but it cannot be. She is a hopeless case; it is judgement against her, instead of the tower of her pride, that has heaped up to heaven. **What does 51:10 mean (cf 51:24; 51:34-37)?** The ruin of Babylon is a sure evidence of God's paternal favour towards His Church. God's people are vindicated not of their own sins but with regards to their enemies. God has punished the Jews as they deserve. They are vindicated in the sense that their grievances against the Babylonians are upheld, as they are cruel tyrants and wicked robbers. The cause, then, of the chosen people is just, with regard to their enemies. Therefore even though they have been used as God's hammer and weapon of war to break nations in pieces (v20-23), *I will repay Babylon and all the inhabitants of Chaldea before your very eyes for all the evil that they have done in Zion, declares the* LORD (v24).

The trustworthiness of Jeremiah's words stems from who God is. Therefore to convince people, Jeremiah points people to look to God. **Who is God according to 51:15-19?** Having faith in God (Mark 11:22) is to hold fast to the faithfulness of God. He is the God that made the world, so there is nothing too hard for Him to do. He continues to have command over all His creation. Idols are a mere sham and cannot frustrate the accomplishment of His word. They are incomparable to the one true God. At the appointed time, they will perish. Jacob however is different because God has chosen them to be His special people for His inheritance.

See how (51:38-40) is fulfilled in Dan 5. **What was taking place on the night when Babylon fell (Dan 5:1-4 & 30)?** The king made a great feast for a thousand of his lords and drank wine in front of the thousand. They defiled temple vessels brought from Jerusalem which they used to serve the wine. That probably was an orgy.

There are many descriptions that God will come down on Babylon harsh. The destruction will be great and she will lay waste – it will be levelled to the ground and all their labour will be futile (v41-58). **What are God's words to His people (51:45-46**

cf 51:6 & 50:8)? God's wrath against Babylon will be fierce and violence is in the land and the fall is sudden (v8) but His people should not be fearful or their hearts be faint. Rather, it is the cue that they are free to go out of her midst. **Is it the end of Babylon (51:62)?** Yes. **What does the sign mean (51:63-64 cf Rev 18:21)?** In Rev, a mighty angel cast a great millstone into the sea, saying, *So will Babylon the great city be thrown down with violence, and will be found no more.* In the sign, it was the stone that sunk the book. But in the thing signified, it was rather the book that sunk the stone. It is the divine sentence passed upon Babylon in this prophecy that sinks that city, which seems unbreakable as a stone. Those that sink under the weight of God's wrath and curse sink irrecoverably. We have now completed the prophecy of Jeremiah.

II.   The historical narrative of the fall of Jerusalem (Ch. 52)

Is the concluding chapter out of place? Why? These were the events that Jeremiah had been prophesying from the beginning of his ministry. A historical record of its fulfilment is a neat way to organise what has been covered in his prophecies. It is also apt in that Jeremiah's prophecy had been proven right and he was a true prophet. Jeremiah was an unusual prophet in that he lived through what he prophesied, and this book clearly is prophecy interwoven with history. It also serves to link up the prophecy to the next book which is Lamentation on the fall of Jerusalem.

A summary: The record starts at the beginning of Zedekiah's reign, which turned very bad in God's sight. Sinning resulted in God's anger and His casting them out of His presence (v1-3). The siege of Jerusalem was triggered by Zedekiah's rebellion and lasted 18 months. Famine was caused by human factor (the siege) rather than a natural disaster. There was a breach in the wall. Zedekiah tried to escape but was overtook and captured. The city was burnt down including the temple. Apart from people, they also pillaged the temple. The ruling class was executed.

Why do you think much attention is given to the pillage of the temple (Ezra 1:7-11)? The temple was the identity of Judah. It shattered their dream of "their return" in a short period of time. The vessels were carefully documented as being taken. They shall be returned after the captivity with the people.

The detailed description of the two pillars (52:21-23) is given in 1 Kings 7:13-22. **What were the names of the pillars (1 Kings 21)?** These pillars were not for support but ornament and significance. They were hollow. *Jachin* means *He will establish* and *Boaz* means *In him is strength*. The Babylonians demolished the walls round Jerusalem (v14) and pulled down the pillars (v17). It symbolised that God had departed from both their civil and spiritual life. No walls can protect, no pillars can sustain those whom God has withdrawn His presence. This is sad.

52:31-34: Jehoiachin was the second last king of Judah who ruled for only 3 months. He was taken in the second deportation. The narrative picked up from where Jehoiachin had spent 37 years in prison. **What do we learn about life from Jehoiachin's fate?** New king makes new rules. The world keeps changing. Prosperity and adversity can turn suddenly. While there is life there is hope that fortune may turn in our favour and quite unexpectedly. Therefore, it is not in vain for those who are under oppression to hope and quietly wait for the salvation of God and the timing is in God's hand.

Questions for your reflection:

Recount His faithfulness in character (e.g. 51:15-19) and to you. Praise Him.

Contemplate the great effort God has to make to pluck you out of the grip of Babylon. Consider Christ. Give thanks.

REFLECTIONS FOR DISCUSSION

Summary of my journey through Jeremiah

(You are encouraged to write your own.)

I first read through Jeremiah 17 years into my Christian life when I made my first attempt to read through the Bible cover to cover. It was an unforgettable experience when the Spirit spoke through Jeremiah then to convict me of being a whore! I dodged Him when He first thundered the conviction at me. I looked left and right, denying that He was speaking to me. But as I progressed through Jeremiah, He only spoke louder and louder, until I could not deny Him anymore. I came from a pagan family and there was ample room to err on spiritual adultery but the charge the Spirit brought on me referred to a very specific incident committed 12 years prior. I could have mustered up excuses in self-defence for that occasion but they were all undone when I was confronted by the holiness of God. *If you, O LORD, should mark iniquities, O Lord, who could stand? But with you there is forgiveness, that you may be feared* (Psalm 130:3). This was exactly what happened on that occasion. When summoned by God in judgement, our mouths are but stopped! Yet once we confess our sins, forgiveness is ready to restore peace.

Thunders and comforts are experienced in one stroke;

114

how blessed we are that we will never taste the full wrath of God because Christ in our stead has drunk the *full* cup – He made sure of it, for example, by refusing the wine mixed with myrrh that was offered to Him (Mark 15:23). If we have never heard the thunders, will we appreciate the depth of Christ's love for us? As we gasp at the horror of the sword, famine and pestilence that befell Judah and at the vivid description of hell, the judgement on Judah that we have walked through via the viewpoint of Jeremiah gives us a physical idea of how the cup of God's wrath may taste like (Ch. 25). It is not hard to imagine the horror when images of wars and descriptions of atrocities have been constantly flashing on our screens in this digital age. The skyline of dwellings is flattened in war-torn cities; the vibrant colours of life yesterday has turned charcoal from burning, sparked off by shelling, the power of destruction that has ripped through man's construction, leaving gaping apertures staring down a wasteland groaning like the hollow sockets haunting in the heaps of skulls singing the anthem of DEATH and HELL with corpses bearing the silent witness of suffering and anguish unspeakable. Do we need any more graphic descriptions of the devastation awaiting mankind if not for what Christ has done for us on the cross? Marvel at the cross and it will bring us to see the unfathomable depth in awe, the source of all comforts.

Where is hope among the rubble? We have to look up for the eternal hope that God has given us. God's Word defines our reality, not our perceived circumstances. Calvin challenges us to live with one foot raised, ready for heaven. Faith means to live in the reality and certainty of heaven in the present. G. R. Evans writes on St. Augustine's City of God: *He encourages people to think big, to look up, beyond the advantage of the present moment, and to form the habit of setting what they do in the context of eternity.*[2] But while this habit is observed in the senior members at church, they will tell us that it has been lost down the generations. Is this

---

[2] St. Augustine, *City of God*, Penguin Classics, 2003, Introduction, p. lvii.

an indication that secular Christianity, a point raised in Session 8, has insidiously crept into our mindset, and in turn in our churches and teaching? Losing that perspective of future glory and joy, we would struggle more in this life to endure unjust suffering, overcome worldliness, make sense of senselessness and respond well to loss and death. It is therefore helpful to journey through Jeremiah when our horizon is stretched to eternity, with the fall of Babylon foretold that spells the end of all opposition to Christ's rule.

Obedience of convenience is no real obedience. Do the Rechabites shame us too? Judah's ongoing hypocrisy with all its subtleties has been soul-searching. Their egregious disobedience climaxed in Chs. 42-44 has stunned me. The chilling end of the bad figs has shocked me equally. I pray for mercy upon our nation, whose acts of disobedience are getting bolder.

Jeremiah is a book of prophecy mixed with historical narratives, whereby prophecy and its fulfilment happened at the same time. Experiencing the fulfilment of his prophecy brought Jeremiah deep sorrow of its devastation and not joy from being proven right, echoing that God has no pleasure in the death of anyone and entreats people to *turn and live* (Eze 18: 23, 32). He was honest and transparent with his physical and emotional struggles. He has taught me about the grief and loneliness of a watchman. That he poured his heart and soul into his ministry to his people who hated him and never failed to disappoint him has also moved me. How he never compromised God's message but always spoke the truth challenges us all. In so many ways, he reminded me of Christ on earth. The tender loving care of the Father in nurturing the spiritual growth of Jeremiah to fulfil his calling and how He was faithful in delivering Jeremiah from all sticky situations is an encouragement to our personal faith walk.

Key themes for general discussion (suggestive and not exhaustive):

1. **The temple is one of the focal points of Jeremiah. How has the study of Jeremiah enriched your understanding of *the temple* in NT?**

   God's desire and intention to dwell with His people is never changed. When He made the heavens and earth, He established the Garden of Eden as His earthly sanctuary to dwell with Adam and Eve. But when sins enter the world, the Holy God needed a designated holy place in order to dwell among His people. First it was the tabernacle. Then centuries later Solomon built the temple as a more permanent place for God to dwell. With the temple destroyed by the Babylonians, God's dwelling place among the people was no more and His presence was withdrawn. When the people returned from exile, they rebuilt the temple under the leadership of Zerubbabel and Jeshua. God promised Zerubbabel that "the latter glory of this house shall be greater than the former" (Hag 2:9). This was fulfilled when the Word became flesh and tabernacle among us." Jesus is the true temple, the place where God dwells with His people. All who joins Him by faith into His body "are being built together into a dwelling place for God by the Spirit" (Eph 2:22). We are like "living stones" being built up as a spiritual house, to be a holy priesthood, to offer spiritual sacrifices acceptable to God through Jesus Christ (1 Peter 2:5). Jesus is the temple, and as our bodies are members of Christ, our bodies is a temple of the Holy Spirit within us. *You are not your own, for you were bought with a price. So glorify God in your body* (1 Cor 6:15, 19-20). We have something very precious in us.

2. **What have you learnt about the OT identity of Messiah?**

Spotlights were put on the king, the false prophets and priests in failing their duties as the shepherds of God's people. They themselves were evil and corrupt in God's sight. As a result, the people were scattered and preyed on by oppressors. Jesus has three offices, the King of kings, the Prophet and the High Priest.

In the Davidic covenant (2 Sam 7:12-16), God promised David that his line will not be broken and his descendant will rule over an everlasting kingdom. He is the "righteous branch" prophesied in Jeremiah 23:5, who "shall reign as king and deal wisely, and shall execute justice and righteousness in the land." He is the Prophet representing God to His people, as He is God the Father manifested. He is now the High Priest in the Holy of the Holies interceding on behalf of the people to God.

3. **In what ways has the study of Jeremiah deepened your understanding of human sinfulness?**

Sin is not a private matter, but always has a corporate dimension to it. If we are not for Christ, we are against Him. God sees our unrelenting sins as joining a conspiracy to overthrow His kingdom (11:9). Neutrality does not exist.

I have also learnt how the law is necessary in defining "sin". The concept of iniquity as being crookedness in our nature is particularly interesting. This is shown by the Jews bending God's law to accommodate and cover their depravity. We see hypocrisy in the gospels when Jesus confronted it.

It is not about the acts but the hearts. Outwardly we could be doing what God expects of us but if it is with a heart against Him, out of hatred rather than love of Him, it is an abomination to Him. How God takes offence from the chanting of "the burden of the Lord" in 23:33-40 is shocking to me.

Blessings could do us harm if we put our faith in the gifts rather than God. It is very convicting.

Idolatry and sin are folly but we are still stuck in it.

One truth against many errors just like what we have. The untruth can afford to accommodate many truths but not the one true Truth.

The stubborn nature of our sinfulness is displayed clearly. We cannot save ourselves and need a new covenant.

4. **How has your knowledge of God deepened by the study?**
    He is sovereign over all things, His people as well as heathens.

    The scandalous love of God for His adulterous people.

    We may learn parenting skill from God in how to rebuke our children in our care. In particular, He reasons with them. Rebuke and discipline are educational to the children about their sins.

    God is long suffering when He corrects us persistently.

    We learn about His justice and how we are inexcusable. We have much more light than the people in OT. He does not need our approval but in His judgement, we see the glory of His justice.

    His grace is a double edged sword – if it does not free us, it is going to condemn us more and more, making us more inexcusable in opposing Him.

5. **What aspects of the gospel do you see in a fresh light?**
    The enormous effort required to pluck us up from our slavery is painted by how formidable Babylon is as an enemy. This operation outshines the significance of Exodus in the mouths of the Jews.

    The vivid image of hell!!

    The human counterparts of Christ's three offices and how they all fail and its consequences

6. **What do you learn about Christian walk from the study of Jeremiah and from his personal walk?**

    All of life worship is not a NT concept. It has been a consistent expectation of God from the beginning (7:8-15).

    Teaching obedience using the Rechabites to contrast that of the Jews is astonishing (Ch. 35). It makes the people's disobedience inexcusable. It also highlights that obedience is from love and not hatred. Even if they perform outward obedience but see God's as the burden of the Lord (23:33-40), this is not true obedience.

    How to live as an exile on earth in this life (Ch. 29).

    In Christian walk, go forward and not backward, unlike the Israelites (7:24). We need to guard against apostasy.

    Heart and soul are poured into ministry besides head knowledge like Jeremiah even towards enemies.

    His boldness – not to compromise God's message, not hold back any word given by God, stay faithful, trusting God with personal safety

    Be on guard against false teaching. What is required?

    How much Jeremiah resembles Christ – His servants are expected to suffer as their Master. We all bear His image and are like Him in some ways. In hard time then, we are comforted for we look to Him and see how He as the first fruit has overcome. This draws us closer to Him.

7. **Has it spoken directly to you and brought on changes in your life?**

    Repentance and gratefulness for my salvation

    Be on guard against false teaching.

    How to speak boldly of the Lord's truth

    Prayer is a gift – it is such a horror when God asks Jeremiah not to pray for his people

    Worship – all of life obedience and not just outward rites.

Printed in Great Britain
by Amazon

82413202R00078